WHY YOU ARE
WHO YOU ARE

WHY YOU ARE WHO YOU ARE
A Psychic Conversation

Graham Bernard

DESTINY BOOKS
NEW YORK

Destiny Books
377 Park Avenue South
New York, New York 10016

Copyright © 1985 Graham Bernard

10 9 8 7 6 5 4 3 2 1

LIBRARY OF CONGRESS CATALOGING IN PUBLICATION DATA

Bernard, Graham.
  Why you are who you are.

  Conversations with a spiritual guide named Richard.
  1. Spirit writings. I. Richard (Spirit) II. Title.
BF130.B417   1985   133.9'3   85-15964
ISBN 0-89281-100-5 (pbk.)

Destiny Books is a division of
Inner Traditions International, Ltd.

Produced and designed by Studio 31.
Typography by Royal Type.

Printed and bound in the United States of America.

Contents

To my wife, Madeleine,
whose contribution and cooperation
have made this book possible

Introduction

As I consider how to begin an accounting of twenty years of psychic communication, I realize what an enormous debt my wife, Madeleine, and I owe to the Whites, Stewart and Betty. *The Betty Book*, written by Stewart Edward White, a writer known previously for his adventure stories, was our first contact with the phenomenon of spirit communication. Up to this time we had had no interest in the subject and had never approached it from any standpoint. When a friend who was an enthusiastic believer talked us into reading this book, we were amazed to find that the Whites seemed to be perfectly normal people, not strange or peculiar at all! In fact, they seemed very much like ourselves.

Their approach was sane, down to earth, and they seemed like friends to us—sensible people, working themselves through an extraordinary experience. We were very struck by Betty's "excursions into the world of other-consciousness," and talked about it among our friends, one of whom was an editor at E. P. Dutton, White's publishers. This was in the sixties, and all of the White books had been published back in the thirties and forties, and were by then out of print with the exception of *The Unobstructed Universe*. Our friend was able to provide us with stray copies of all of the books, and our lives were changed. We were intrigued by the discoveries that Betty made through mental mediumship and found ourselves eager to experiment to see if we, too, could succeed at communicating with the "unobstructed universe."

Because the Whites had begun their early communication on the Ouija board, we decided to try it. Although we felt somewhat ridiculous, with our board purchased in the children's games department at Macy's department store, we were amazed at the dispatch with which it got to work.

We immediately found ourselves in touch with someone who identified herself as "Teach," the name by which I had known my deceased former voice teacher, Frances. She was a remarkable woman who had influenced my thinking on many subjects. I recall her once remarking that some children seemed like old souls and some like young souls—an idea I had accepted because it came from her, but hadn't thought about too seriously at the time.

"Teach" provided us with evidential information about herself that coincided with what I knew about Frances, except for one thing. She said she had had four children, but I had only known three. However, upon checking this out with a mutual friend, I learned that her first child had died. In addition to these assurances, I felt intuitively that it was indeed Frances who was communicating with us.

Her objective was to get us *off* the Ouija board and into other forms of communication. I soon started with automatic writing, which developed almost immediately into what Frances called brain impingement. I remember the first day, standing at the piano, pen in hand, arm free so that it could be moved easily, waiting expectantly. I didn't have to wait more than a moment before the fingers that held the pen began to tingle (this had also happened the first time I touched the pointer on the Ouija board). The pen moved, first in circles, then in interlocking ovals along the paper, like those we used to form as children in penmanship class. I soon developed a feeling that there was something for me to learn from this initial experience, which had to be grasped before we could proceed. I had to develop the inner freedom to let the pen move freely, not to hold back out of fear or timidity, but rather go with it in spirit and let the communication happen through me. This was something I only sensed at first; the understanding came later. With this understanding, sentences developed.

At first the pen moved slowly but firmly, and then, little by little, the pace picked up and I found my hand writing sentences. At this time the words and sentences were all run together. The free, rounded movement seemed to be the essential element. I never knew what I had written until after the pen stopped moving and I was able to read it, separating each word with a short vertical line. I worked in this way for a brief period each day.

Then, one day, I suddenly realized that I was not just writing words in an automatic manner; I was hearing the words, or rather, the words came to me in thought and I found myself writing, with my own handwriting, words that I already knew or thought. The transition was so subtle that it took me a little while to grasp what was happening, and it was only when I was no longer running the words together, but separating them and writing them down as they came to me, that the transition was made clear. At this point Frances explained that she was impinging her thoughts on my brain and that this was how I was receiving the words.

When this phase of the development was completed, Frances told me that she wanted me to work with Richard, a friend of ours who had been killed in World War II. Richard and I had both studied with Frances and had become close through our shared interest in singing. He died as a young ensign in a seemingly freak

accident aboard an aircraft carrier. While standing
watch, he was shot down by inadvertent machine gun
fire as a plane was landing. His untimely death had been
a source of great sorrow to me. I was bereft of a true
friend whom I had loved like a brother.

If I were to describe Richard in one word, it would be
"goodness." He was very like the mythical character of
Parsifal, the "perfect fool," a combination of naiveté and
wisdom, simplicity and purity of heart, with laughing
blue eyes and curly blond hair. His death had left an
emptiness in me. And now Frances was saying that
Richard and I were going to be together again! My life
would be complete! Or so I thought (I had a lot to learn).
Richard had a project in mind concerning life and how
to live it. Needless to say, I welcomed the opportunity to
rekindle an old friendship and learn how to overcome
my problems as well.

Since that time, the summer of 1964, both my wife
and I have been in communication with Richard
through brain impingement, each of us working on
different projects, sometimes helping each other and
sometimes going our own ways.

A great deal of time was devoted to establishing the
groundwork for an understanding of what Richard
wanted us to know. I spent no more than one hour a day
on communication, and much of it consisted of
Richard's efforts to help me recognize and overcome my
emotional problems. I was also teaching a full day of
voice lessons during this period and trying to handle the
vicissitudes of raising three daughters, maintaining a
New York brownstone, and building a house in the
country.

It wasn't until 1980, when Richard decided that our
channel of communication was deeply enough grooved
to insure absolute accuracy, that he said we were ready

to write this book, the first of six projected volumes. I worked alone on it, receiving the material for an hour each day for two years, and organizing it during the following year.

What follows is the result of my efforts, with my wife's advice and Richard's persistence, and is intended as counsel in the business of living here and now. The premise of the material is Richard's and the content comes from him. The advice and guidance over the years were at first intended for me alone. The subjects discussed were clarifications of and solutions to problems of mine. But this later material proved to be of universal value.

This, then, is a summation of what I have learned about life and how it should be lived. The precepts have helped me a great deal in living my own life more constructively (I discuss this in more detail in the Postscript). I pass them on with the hope that they may prove valuable to you, too, in discovering why you are who you are and in realizing your own potential.

Crucial Concepts

One day, as I watched a friend of mine embroidering a wall hanging of Egyptian hieroglyphics in earth colors, I remarked that the design the characters made was very attractive, and I asked whether she knew what they meant. "Yes." she replied, "it says, 'It isn't easy to be a person.'" We laughed, and I added that it was interesting that people of an ancient civilization felt much the same as we do about life and its problems.

It wasn't until Richard and I had been communicating for some time, comparing the conditions of our lives (minutiae to satisfy my curiosity), that he suddenly said, "Today I want to start to help you with your problems."

"What do you mean?" I asked.

"I want to teach you how to live you life to the best advantage. The reason for this will become clear as we proceed."

Suddenly recalling the Egyptian motto, I said, "It isn't easy to be a person." Richard agreed and told me that he intended to help me see why this was true and also help me learn how to make things easier for myself—and even to understand the purpose of life itself. But before we were to proceed, he wanted me to understand and absorb some basic terminology and concepts. "Think about this," he continued, and recited this series of statements:

Reincarnation is a fact.

Immortality is a reality.

Our goal is perfection, that is, to become perfectly individual and perfectly at-one with God as well.

You are where you are because you want to be there.

You have come prepared to cope with your problems.

Overcoming your faults is essential to your growth.

Growth is the essence of life.

Perfection is its culmination.

"Hold on!" I said, overwhelmed by the flood of new ideas. "I couldn't get past that first statement, let alone the last one."

He responded, "Of course. I just want you to get the idea that we are not going to spend our time on chit-chat."

Reincarnation and immortality were familiar concepts, but how about, "You are where you are because you want to be there" and "You have come prepared to cope"? I considered these hard to swallow. Even the ancients found it hard to be a person, and things are certainly no easier now!

Richard seemed pleased with my balking. But he said it would help me to ask the proper questions so that I could learn what he wanted me to know. Finally, I agreed to settle down and listen. In fact, listening has become my chief occupation for over twenty years. I have been constantly admonished, "Concentrate on listening. Don't try for concepts. Listen for words. Stay away from thought. Listen. Listen to hear my words, one at a time." What I've heard has affected my life so unquestionably for the good that I want to share the information with others. This is my wish and Richard's wish.

Before I recount our conversation, I would like to pre-

pare the reader for certain crucial concepts which
Richard refers to in the book. These, then, are the crucial concepts:

1. *The nature of God's being is truth.* As creations of
   God, we must try to comprehend truth.
2. *The nature of God's will is construction.* If we are to
   do God's will, we must live constructive lives.
3. *The nature of God's love is creative harmony.* We
   must learn to emulate this state.
4. *The nature of self-will is deterrence.* Through self-
   will, our development may be deterred. However,
   deterrence does not mean destruction, for nothing
   created is ever destroyed; it merely changes form.
5. *The Place of Preparation* is the place from which we
   come and to which we go between incarnations.
   This place is home for a very long time.
6. *The elements of development* are the particular
   circumstances of an incarnation, brought about
   fundamentally by our choice of parents.
7. *Our spiritual equipment consists of love, sense of
   truth, and intuition.* This is the equipment we
   bring with us from the Place of Preparation. It is
   used in coping with growth problems during our
   lives on earth.
8. *The quality-quantity factors* are basic to the
   functioning of an incarnation. A quality (such as a
   virtue) developed in the Place of Preparation can
   become permanent only by being lived out in quantity during an incarnation.
9. *Intent* is the plan of a life, the potential goal of an
   incarnation.
10. *An event* is the culmination of converging circum-
    stances that influence the outcome of an incarna-
    tion.
11. *Karma* is the working out of moral law. Every

wrong that we commit must be paid for in some way.

12. *Thoughts are things.* That is, they have concrete reality and power to influence events. Constructive thought contributes to construction as a force at large. Deterrent thought contributes to deterrence as a force at large.

13. God, Who is the All in All, is perceived as a loving parent, *God the Father.*

At the end of the book, I present a summary of the truths that Richard has imparted in the conversations which follow.

The Place of Preparation

To help get our conversation started, Richard suggested I pick a topic that interested me. When I thought about the idea that we come to earth prepared to cope with our problems, I realized that the Place of Preparation is very important for all of us, since it must provide us with the coping skills we need before returning to earth.

Tell me about the Place of Preparation.
We all spend a great deal of our time in this place. It is a realm close to earth. It occupies the same place as earth, but on a higher frequency. This place is our home during the entire reincarnation cycle, where we acquire all the qualities needed for our development, which must be given quantity through living on earth. Development influences the way we see things here. As we are able to generate higher frequencies within ourselves, we become more capable of seeing things as they really are. Such development is obvious in our appearance. Thoughts are things, and here we are able to create any sort of environment through thought, to suit the needs of the moment.

The Place of Preparation is of great importance to you on earth, because it is from here that all communication originates. I am in this place whenever I communicate with anyone on earth. It is with the power of thought that we travel here, and no matter where I am, I can be in

5

the Place of Preparation instantly by just thinking myself there. Distance is a matter of frequency on this side:
the higher the frequency, the higher the realm. One
manifestation of development is the ability to manipu-
late frequency. As we first attempt to experience the
conditions which the higher frequency brings about, we
find that just as we have difficulty adjusting to higher
altitudes on earth, so do we have difficulty sustaining
the frequency required in the higher realms. Development brings this ability about. But now we are talking
about the Place of Preparation.

Is this where everyone goes at death?
No. Those who have earned this place through their
achievements on earth come to the Place of Preparation.
The greater percentage do come here, but this is not the
only place by any means. Those who have completed the
need for the reincarnation cycle go on into other, more
advanced states, where they are able to continue their
development. There are those, too, who no longer need
the reincarnation cycle but who deliberately return to
help in specific ways. The benefactors of mankind are
usually these. When they die, they return to the heights
they have achieved. Those who have done themselves
harm during an incarnation may find themselves in a
dank, murky atmosphere, unable to see because there is
no light at all, just the mire of inertia and indolence.
This place is called the Lower Region because of the
extremely low frequency which exists there. Overpowering lassitude permeates the atmosphere, making it difficult to bring about change.

What is the atmosphere of the Place of Preparation?
The atmosphere is impossible to express accurately. It
would be like asking someone whose sight had been

restored after life-long blindness to describe how azure blue looks. Nothing fades or dies here. Everything is at the peak of perfection and remains so. The air is charged with vitalizing electricity, which energizes with each breath. A supreme feeling of well-being permeates everyone. Vital color abounds. There is a constant awareness of pervading love, which warms and energizes all. The flowers and trees give off musical sounds as they respond to the admiration bestowed on them. Matter is of a different substance, both lacking solidity and tougher at the same time. There are no obstructions. When we come upon an object, we just pass through it and go on our way; there is no need to go around anything. Thought is the activating power. If we want to go from point A to point B, we just think ourselves there, and we are there. We are taught all we need to know about getting around, and with little effort we find ourselves functioning freely.

There is tremendous exhilaration at first in our new-found abilities, but it soon becomes second nature and is taken for granted. The ability to function is to a great degree a matter of recall, since we've been able to do this many times before. Each time we return, our memory returns more quickly until such time as we no longer need the reincarnational cycle. From this point on, the facility is permanent.

This is not a police state in any form. No one is watching or checking on us. Here we feel part of a perfect whole. The joy we experience is overwhelming at first, but as we understand more and more, we realize that this is just a part of God's will for us all.

Since there is no sex, love is experienced in quite different ways. In the act of love, two entities come together and intermingle in an ecstatic state. Although emotional and psychological elements are shared as they are in the sexual act, the actual state is quite different from a sexual experience in that the two actually become one entity in the process.

Is food necessary in the Place of Preparation?

No, it is not necessary at all. But there is an experience parallel to the enjoyment of food and drink for those who so choose. Since our bodies are everlasting by nature, they need no sustenance to maintain them.

Can you describe your body to me?

Well, it would be very difficult. I will say, however, that I would be recognizable to you were you to see me now, because what you would see would be the essential spiritual elements you would know to be me. My color might surprise you, but you would surely know me.

Is sleep essential?

No. We never experience fatigue. It is always possible, though, to create a quiet place for meditation whenever we feel the need. Everyone understands these things here, and we may do as we wish any time.

If everyone creates his or her own environment, are there as many places as people?

The answer is yes and no. We are drawn to a particular place because of our development, our loved ones, and our desires. Within that environment, however, we can create our own special places, maybe a place like one we have known or a place of pure fantasy, or maybe a place that represents stability, security, or any other condition for which we may have need. This particular environment can change at will as our desires and needs change. Those of us who choose to stay in the safe, beautiful environment we have created are removed from the feeling of movement which permeates the atmosphere. The air itself seems to say, "Let's go. Move forward. Get on with it!" Even though we may seal our-selves off from this and choose to remain in an environ-ment which suits our needs as we see them, sooner or later we come to realize that the perfection we have established is no longer satisfying; we must break out and seek help to understand our developing unrest. This is a most important moment because it allows us to open ourselves up to the reality which surrounds us and respond to it constructively. When this happens and we realize we don't need our own environment, we are no longer isolated in it and move freely within the environ-ment as a whole. We are visited by loved ones and teachers and advisers, and even when we make sojourns out into the world, so to speak, we always have the comfort of our special place to come back to. Total free-dom is a learning process.

How do you learn to adjust to your new environment?
We learn the trick from those who specialize in the development of mobility and imagination. This is es-sential to understanding the environment as a whole, how to get around in it, and how to create a special place which will help to keep a sense of identity. Disorienta-tion is a major problem to newcomers, so learning about our new talents, which are a part of our new being, gives security. Even though we may be surrounded by loved ones, this new experience is difficult to relate to. Once we master the fundamentals, we feel more at home, and from then on integration gradually becomes total. There is no typical case, however, since there are no two situa-tions exactly alike. Some find it very difficult to adjust. Others feel at home right away. It all depends on develop-ment and purpose.

You describe your world in wonderful terms, but since everyone sees it differently, isn't this just your vision of what exists?

No. What I am describing to you is as it really is and as it is apparent to the enlightened. Those who do not see it this way haven't yet developed their new faculties or come to understand the place fully. We all come with the potential to understand and visualize its true beauty. It takes time and development. No one is here who shouldn't be here. Many need a great deal of development before true enlightenment comes, but they have the capacity or they wouldn't be here.

If we find it difficult to adjust to a place even when we have earned it, what makes us eligible?

If we have achieved a measure of development during an incarnation, if we have managed to respond to at least a portion of the circumstances of our lives constructively, then we have realized growth. Some of us realize a great deal, others little, but all have a right to go to the Place of Preparation. Here we learn what we have already accomplished and what we have yet to accomplish. Those who reincarnate primarily to help others, to aid in important causes for mankind or to reveal truth, don't need the earth experience for themselves, but return as a source of inspiration. This experience advances them to even higher realms than those they left. They have no need for the Place of Preparation at all.

If growth is apparent in this place, do problems show up too?

No. Development is apparent through color. However, the elements which comprise the development or color are not evident in themselves. Here we are freed from our problems so we can concentrate on construction. We are aware we have such problems because we are informed of them. We can tell by appearances just how developed we are. We are provided with all the learning facilities needed plus any number of people to help and advise us. The atmosphere is conducive to learning, and after we have become free from the need to establish an environment which makes us comfortable, we are able to appreciate what has been provided.

Is the Place of Preparation the only realm from which the earth is contacted?

Yes. The frequency of this place allows contact with the frequency of earth without difficulty, although there are frequencies which are closer to the earth frequency. They are occupied by those who are unwilling to free themselves from earth ties. Many undeveloped souls reside there also, not knowing who they are or where they are, trying to get ahead at the expense of others. After death, most people pass through this region on their way to the Place of Preparation. However, there are those who are attracted to it through their strongly developed, unresolved compulsions and remain there trying to satiate the insatiable. Others stay close to the earth because of the strong emotional pulls and often appear as ghosts, poltergeists, and the like. They are trying to make amends for past wrongs, not realizing they have changed through death.

Has God's plan failed for such undeveloped souls?

No. These people are visited by teachers who try to show them the way out of their dilemma, and indeed, some do find their way back. However, the difficulties are great and the task is arduous. These are not the Lower Regions. That is still another place. The Lower Regions are for developed souls who have deliberately chosen deter-

rence in the face of everything and have knowingly de-
fied God's will. These people are those who have never
developed understanding and have sought self-gain and
gratification as the end of all being. Such people become
victimized by insatiable desire and lust. Self-gratification is their aim at the expense of all else.

What do we learn in the Place of Preparation?

We learn who we are, why we exist, where we have been,
and where we are going. Everything necessary is available to those of us who are preparing to reincarnate.
There is nothing we cannot find in the way of help. If, on
the other hand, we are in no hurry to move on, we can
stay indefinitely. The decision is up to us. Even though
we may be holding up our development, we are not
encouraged in any way to change our minds. However,
in spite of this, the impetus to move on is ever present,
and everyone is affected by it sooner or later. Those who
want to understand themselves, their reason for being,
life in general, and so on, are able to do so by examining
the records of their past lives, which they may peruse to
their hearts' content. With the opportunity to discover
all about our lives, our true nature, development needs
and potential, we are allowed to discover ourselves from
our beginnings. All of our past lives and the details of
those lives are recorded, and the information is made
available. We learn how we have dealt with our problems
in past lives and what that shows about our acquired
qualities, our stage of development; what is lacking as
well as what has been achieved. This information is
essential to learning how to take the next step, but none
of it is given unless we ask for it. No information is
forced on us. It is provided in accordance with our needs
as we see them.

　　To be able to read a detailed account of one's entire life

experience is rewarding in many ways. At first we are
overwhelmed by the truth. But when we recover, we
have insight from which to consider future steps. Once
the information is absorbed (and it is a very private
experience), we are given the opportunity to share our
feelings and problems with others who are wiser and
more developed (this fact is obvious here), so we can find
firm ground on which to build. The purpose of experience is growth, and growth is our most important concern. It helps us to understand what has gone before in
order to see the developing patterns. It is easier to plan
our next move if we understand the ways in which we
resolved previous attempts to move forward.

*Is there a specific length of time most of us stay in the
Place of Preparation?*
No. We might stay a few years in your time or thousands
of years. It depends upon the complexity of the problems
we want to solve and/or the quality or qualities we want
to acquire, or whether we want to think about growth at
all. We do have eternity, but we must decide at what
degree of advancement we want to spend our time.
Working to resolve problems and realize goals is very
rewarding wherever you are. Our lives are intended to
augment the Godhead, so there may be, in the ultimate
state, a multiplicity of being which is integral to the
whole—oneness and individuality multiplied endlessly
in a state of perfection. The one purpose our lives serve
is to develop to this ultimate state so that we, as individuals, can become a part of the perfect whole which
is God. Attention has been paid to all particulars of this
most magnificent of dreams, and the Place of Preparation is a very important part of it. It is the feeding ground
for all those who want to be a part of the plan. Here is
where we learn the lessons which must be put into

practice elsewhere before they are realized. Here is where we can renew ourselves and are given a glimpse of the extent of God's love for us all. Here is where we can feel close to the Being of Whom we hope to become an integral, functioning part some day.

Just how important is the Place of Preparation?

It is the most influential realm for us during our entire reincarnational cycle. It is home for a great deal of our eternal life. It is the first step on the stairway to paradise. It is the place where we first understand the extent of God's plan and our part in it. It is our first home in heaven, and we have stored-up memories which add to our enjoyment and appreciation of it with each trip back. Here is where we meet our loved ones with whom we share a common bond, to whom we are most closely related, with whom we share the same final goal, and who, with us, will become integral parts of a larger Being, parts of God, uniquely individual and uniquely at-one with Him. Here is where we are able to learn what we need to know of the mysteries of the universe and our common bond with all living matter. This is the most important place for all who want to share in God's dream and ultimately reach perfection.

Many people get hung up on false notions of what heaven is all about and cannot accept that they have farther to go. They believe that this is paradise, the ultimate achievement, with nothing left but peace and quiet. They create their own peace and quiet and live in it with friends of similar mood. However, even they are able to be aware of the activities of others around them if they so choose. They are encouraged to attend classes for their own development. Those who attend out of curiosity often leave confused and insecure. They seek refuge in their "true home" at first, but gradually may come to seek wisdom and choose to stay in the free world. Those who think they have reached the end when they come here have a very difficult problem to overcome. They must learn the importance of growth and its ultimate outcome, but this often takes a very long time and the efforts of many people on their behalf. In many ways their problems are more difficult to overcome than the problems of the deterrent ones, because those who willfully developed a self above all else experience such hardship in the Lower Regions that they are brought to their senses more readily. However, those who have not transgressed woefully and are certain that they are among the chosen few think that they are where they belong, in heaven. A protracted experience of this kind can have the effect of too many chocolate creams, and one can wish for something else in life.

The urge toward growth here is as dominant as the urge of survival on earth, and sooner or later it has its effect on all, even those with deep-seated problems. Those who come here with open minds are light years ahead of those with rigid ideas. On the other hand, the wise ones help by sharing their knowledge and experience with the newcomers who want to learn. This sharing experience is their own particular growth factor of the moment, so it is done with great energy and love.

What happens to us upon arrival?
We are usually met by friends and loved ones who share our feelings and assure us that we are in the right place. This adjustment is sometimes difficult, but love has much to do with its success. Those who have no loved ones to meet them are often at a loss, not certain of just where they are and what has happened. This condition is soon corrected, however, by those advisers who arrive to help them. Depending upon the conditions of death

and the development of the soul, those who arrive after violent death or protracted, difficult illness may need special care to bring their traumatized souls to health. During this period, help is administered in all ways to bring them to normalcy.

We all need time to adjust to our new bodies and the different conditions of life here. We begin to put our new-found abilities into practice, and in due time we learn about our past. What we learn about our previous lives is all-consuming at first. To be confronted with our history and realize how little growth we have earned and to see how far we must go to reach the ultimate seem defeating. But after help has been administered, we begin to see that our immediate goals are within our grasp and they need be our only concern of the moment. If we strive only to get from point A to point B, we need not worry about point Z until we have reached point Y. This realization is comforting, and along with it comes gratitude for what has been accomplished and for the opportunity to continue to learn. The humility we feel at this point brings rewards which will enable us to see more clearly and recognize our real relationship with our Maker, the Mind Who conceived us and made it possible to become as He is.

Those of us who are capable of helping others to see more clearly have earned the privilege through their own efforts. The teachers are those who, by reason of their development, belong in higher realms but return here to earn still further credits toward growth by utilizing what is theirs to help others. They no longer need the earth experience but spend their time here helping us. We are told that similar situations exist in all of the higher realms as well. Those who have reached perfection continue to allow the rest of us the healing and inspiring benefit of their presence from time to time.

God works through people, and this is true right up to the top.

How do we acquire a quality?

Aided by many who are here to help, we are able little by little to acquire the ingredients which comprise a particular quality. With the advice of others and understanding of what we have been able to accomplish in the past, we first set a goal for ourselves. The goal may be simple, like learning patience, or complicated, like ridding ourselves of complex human problems. Its accomplishment may take a long or short period of time, in your terms; comparatively little concentrated effort or a great deal of concentrated effort. Here, time is always in the present. Our goals do not take time to accomplish, just effort. As for the process itself, it is impossible to describe except to say that it is the application of desire power to our needs.

What happens when the goal is accomplished?

We may do one of two things. We may decide to add another quality or we may decide to satisfy the one we have gained by trying the earth experience again. We are given advice if we ask for it, but the decision is ours alone. Reality here is what we make of it. It has many faces and all of them have validity. The essential values remain the same, but the peripheral factors can differ. We remain ourselves no matter where we are, and we must trust and believe this fact. It is essential to learn to rely on ourselves and our inner feelings because these stay with us no matter where we go. The self that we must trust and develop is found in our hearts and expressed through our intuition. These are the permanent elements which become our only source of help during a transition period. Those who have never learned to trust these inner feelings find themselves at a loss when the time comes to make a change. They tend literally to fly apart from fear of the strange, unexpected conditions they are experiencing, and they have few inner resources upon which to rely. This causes confusion and blindness, and great effort on the part of many is required to bring about integration.

The way to prepare for the future is to live fully in the present, knowing that the quality of life we live now produces the product for the future. By learning to trust our spiritual equipment (love, sense of truth, and intuition) we are living according to plan and will reap our rewards, not only on earth but in other realms as well. We know what to depend upon, so we're not fearful of change. Our inner being remains constant in the face of all change. Change, to us, denotes growth. To get on with it is essential. We must welcome change, not fear it, since change is essential in a constantly evolving universe. Our spiritual equipment can provide us with the constant which is necessary if we are to embrace change and achieve growth.

If, as you say, reality there differs according to individual interpretations, how do we arrive at a particular concept of reality?

We are kindred souls to all with whom we have shared love. Our kinship forms a bond of eternal love and devotion which draws us together in a sharing experience. Love shows us the path to travel. Birds of a feather flock together. We, as kindred souls, seek each other out, and our experiences are the outcome of our relationships. This doesn't mean that kindred souls are all at the same stage of development. It means we have related final objectives which draw us together wherever we find ourselves. The more developed ones help the less developed ones. This kinship can never be broken. Relationships vary at each incarnation in order for us to experience more and more of knowing and loving one another. We can be attached to many, many people in this way. When we arrive here again, we feel we are coming home after a sojourn in a foreign country, and we are grateful if we can bring back with us the rewards of our efforts abroad. We look forward to the day when we can leave these travels and troubles behind us.

The basic requirements for growth prevail for all, and we must use these elements in whatever guise we see them. Truth is subject to interpretation, but the various interpretations don't alter the validity of the truth. A beautiful singing tone is heard and interpreted in different ways by all who hear it. But the tone itself is not affected by the scrutiny of others and is enjoyed by all in accordance with their capacity. So it is with truth. What I describe to you is true and can be understood by all. Whether or not it strikes a particular note of harmony depends upon makeup and capacity, but the logic can be understood by all. If the essentials are developed, we benefit in time of need, no matter which side of the fence we find ourselves on.

My hope is that you will make the most of your earthly experience this time, so you will be prepared for what is to come. Bringing this information to you is my growth effort, and I am trying to accomplish it with all of the love and energy I possess. Remember this: effort and reward are the same thing! Our time spent together is for your benefit, my benefit, and the benefit of all those who recognize and follow the truth of what is said.

Reincarnation

I expressed to Richard my thought that from God's point of view, since He is All and Everything, reincarnation wasn't really necessary.

What is the point of God's wanting to augment Himself endlessly if He is already All in All?

God, in his love, conceived the possibility of giving of Himself to create individual entities of life. In this way He brought about all that exists. His desire was to share Himself in such a way that the ecstasy of Godhood could be experienced by endless numbers who could become gods in their own right and yet be at-one with Him. The universe as you know it is only a part of the total concept. Everything that exists in both the incarnate and discarnate worlds is constantly evolving, and this evolution is God's plan. Reincarnation is the plan for the evolution of the spirit, the means through which the human being becomes God. The Godhead, then, is an evolving state and will continue to be so ad infinitum. Even those in the most nearly perfect state continue to evolve. In this way, God is continually augmented.

When we decide to reincarnate, what happens?

In our efforts to find a host (the unborn baby to suit our needs), we consult with the advisers about our goals. There is discussion about the various possibilities and the particular elements of development which are present in each situation. Our needs are assembled, and the conditions best suited to those needs are realized. This

21

information is put through a process which comes up
with multiple-choice solutions. The ramifications of the
possible outcome of each choice are discussed with
advisers. At this point there is no concern about our
readiness. Once we make the decision to reincarnate,
whether or not the advisers agree, they do not attempt to
deter us from this action. By the time we apply for a visa,
so to speak, the trip is already under way. The overriding
concern then is to find the proper circumstances for the
development of our particular needs. The plans of the
lives of possible parents are all laid out and gone over
with a fine-tooth comb. The final choice is concluded
with our decision, based on our own heart feelings.

*Could there be many people competing for the same
parents?*

Yes, but they are not aware of just what the competition
is. The opportunities are always changing as circumstances change. Decisions often must be made with
precision and speed. At conception the spirit visits the
host to establish a bond with the new life. By the fifth
month the applicant makes regular visits to the host to
become acquainted with the new conditions as they
develop. At birth the soul is drawn to the host as though
by a magnet and remains encased in that body for the
entire plan of that life.

*Do we know at this time whether we are going to be
black, white, yellow, or red; rich or poor; intelligent or
stupid; and so on?*

No. What we do know about is the emotional and psychic
development of the parents, whether or not we have
known them before, the particular environment which
will be created by our presence in their midst, and
whether or not this will be good for and helpful to our
purposes.

Why shouldn't we know the other factors too?

Because we must go into this experience with faith and trust that no matter what situation we find ourselves in physically, we are in the right place psychologically. Although we are expected to know all we need to know before we leave, we must exercise the same faith and trust we will need where we are going.

Can we expect our intellectual capacity to reflect our spiritual development?

No, certainly not. Intellectual prowess is not a criterion for spiritual development. In fact, the most developed souls are often very simple people. The intellect can be a detriment to spiritual development because it emphasizes mental capacity and overlooks the value of intuition. The mentally developed person knows because he has learned. The intuitive person just knows.

Mental capacity can be useful to spiritual development if it is kept in its place as a helpful tool. But when it becomes the end-all of life (when technology runs a person's life, for example), it has usurped intuition as the source of our actions and the life of the spirit diminishes. A society which worships technology and admires the so-called self-made man has lost sight of the basic purpose of living, spiritual development. We may be given great intelligence so that it can be used for good; or we may be given great intelligence so that we can probe the mysteries of life; or we may be given great intelligence so that we can turn away from the temptations it offers and learn to live a simple, spiritual life. All of this relates to the particular task we set for ourselves when we decide to reincarnate. If it is a complicated, intricate task, the circumstances of our lives will reflect this. This doesn't necessarily mean we will be given a life fraught with difficulties. Maybe it would be much more complicated and difficult for us to cope with a life of wealth and intelligence. It is much easier to arrive at the understanding which can lead to spiritual enlightenment if one isn't weighed down by too much worldliness. The circumstances of our lives are tailor-made for our spiritual development, no matter how they appear on the surface. Depending upon the particular qualities we want to acquire, the circumstances may develop an environment in which we can grow or one from which we need to separate ourselves.

What equipment do we need to prepare for an incarnation?

Aside from faith in the goodness of God and trust in His will for us, we must make certain that our love, sense of truth, and intuition (our spiritual equipment) are in good order. They are the tools we need to achieve our purpose, and as we demand more from ourselves, our equipment must be up to the task. After we have acquired the essence of a quality which we need, we must be certain that our spiritual equipment is equal to the requirement. When we are sure of this, we are ready to tackle the assignment. Since success or failure, based on our own decisions, is basic to our growth, we are always allowed to test our faculties and learn from the outcome.

If our faults are latent in the Place of Preparation, why don't we see clearly and make the right decisions every time?

Because we are all individuals and see things according to our own development. Deterrence doesn't enter into this. Judgment is what we are talking about. We see the same truths differently at all stages of development, right up to the apex. This is partly what individuality is about, seeing the truth clearly from different points of view. Those of us in the Place of Preparation are far from

perfect to begin with, or we wouldn't be here. Our enthu-
siasms may overshadow our judgment in our desire to
progress. Being well prepared involves a great deal of
practice, a great many incarnations. When we are new at
it, we are less skillful than when we are veterans. There
is a great deal to adjust to here, and newcomers have
difficulty with priorities. We can thank God for the
opportunity to learn through repetition. With evolvement comes perception. It all takes effort to achieve.

**Couldn't the decisions about our reincarnation be
made by the wise ones to assure us of a fulfilled
lifetime?**

Yes, you might think so. But you must remember that
the ultimate decision is made by the applicant alone.
This is the law. These are our lives, and we are responsible for their outcome, given all of the help heaven can
provide. Our uniqueness is protected and developed at
all times by our decisions and ours alone. Although we
could say that a choice of parents need not be difficult if
we are properly prepared, we must not overlook the fact
that there are many people desiring to do the same
thing, and it is very easy to get caught up in the rush.
Proper preparation is the key to success of any kind, and
it is especially true when it comes time to reincarnate.

Relationships figure in the preparation of an incarnation too. This is where the heart feelings come in. We
tend to reincarnate with the same people over and over
again because of the attachments which form in the
process and because of related goals. This is not always
the case, however. Many want to put immediate goals
ahead of relationships and go for the best possible situation regardless. However, there is much to be said for
following our heart feelings because the final associations are based on ultimate goals, and we tend to continue to have varied relationships with the same group of

people, all of whom are headed for the same ultimate
goal. By the time we reach our ultimate goal, we will have
become fused elements of a being of like purpose, which,
in turn, will become an element of the Supreme Being, of
which each of us is an individual, integral part. Kindred
souls are closely related because of this. We are all children of God, but some of us are brothers and sisters and
some of us are just "kissing cousins." A close relationship tends to draw people together and give them a
cohesive sense of identity. (When you realize that the
same person may be your father, mother, sister,
brother, wife, husband, child, lover, or friend in different incarnations, you come to see that in the end the
two of you will have much in common and will become as
one in final realization.) Ultimate goals for each vary
endlessly because of the endless possibilities. Those
with similar ultimate goals are not identical either.
Since there are no two souls alike, their ultimate goals
will not be exactly alike, but will be a part of the whole,
becoming complete only when all of the parts are assembled in a state of perfection. Each makes a unique contribution to the whole, the final, objective being. The
ultimate goal for all is perfection. The ultimate goal for
each is unique at-oneness with God and unique individuality as well.

*Are you saying that the ultimate goal of each of us is
to become an integral part of a greater being, which,
in turn, is a functioning organ of the body of God?*

You have asked a complex question, but since it has
merit, I will say this: each of us has a destiny. That
destiny is to bring cohesion to the perfect state of God.
We are at present unrealized bits and fragments of God,
and ultimately we will become perfect parts in the perfect unity of God. This will be the realization of God's

dream. If construction is God's will, then growth, which is constructive, must be an integral part of God's creation, and we are a part of the creation. Growth is accomplished by setting goals and achieving them. This point is made clear in the Place of Preparation. Here also we learn that perfection is composed of many qualities, all of which must be understood, developed, and earned. They are to be understood and developed in the Place of Preparation and earned in the earth experience. We set about to acquire one or more fundamental qualities which are needed in our present stage of development, and at this point our reincarnational cycle begins.

Goals are necessary for all human beings. The living out of each day makes its contribution, either toward or away from our goal. It may be that we are unaware of the fact that we have set a goal for our present incarnation, but we do know how we feel about our lives and what we would like to accomplish. If, in trying to fulfill ourselves in this way, we live a constructive life, we will indeed reach our goals, whether or not we understand this fact. By following our heart feelings and applying our spiritual equipment (love, sense of truth, and intuition) to the elements of development (environment), we will indeed accomplish what our souls so need and desire.

We have considered immediate goals, but we must recognize that the goal of each incarnation is an integral part of our final goal. Final goals are elements of the ultimate unity of the Godhead. Just as there are elements in our bodies which have specific functions, without which our bodies would not be complete, so the Godhead is composed of specifics which contribute to the whole. Ever since God decided to give of Himself by creating sparks of life, each with its own uniqueness, which He has allowed to grow and become perfect in itself so that perfection would be endlessly augmented,

His dream has been developing and will continue to do so until all has reached fulfillment. In this way all of us will experience our own uniqueness and oneness with God simultaneously; our ultimate goal and God's dream fulfilled.

Are you saying that until that time comes, God is less than perfect?

Certainly not. God is what perfection is. But since God is All in All, by granting us free will, He has made it possible for us to become like Him through our own efforts, and also made Himself a victim of that free will. As long as deterrence exists, we are delaying the outcome of God's gift to us, perfection. All that exists is evolving in accordance with God's will. Our free will allows us to choose between construction (God's will) and deterrence (self-will) and either participate in this evolution or deter it, according to our own thought and action. With the privilege of participation goes the obligation of responsibility. None of us can shirk this and also expect to move forward.

The purpose of all that exists is to develop multiplicity of being, which will augment the possibilities of the ecstasy of perfection endlessly. Before this can happen, each fragment of free will must be aligned with construction in order to reach perfection through its own efforts and become at-one with God. In the Place of Preparation we learn that virtue is a state of being. It is composed of those elements which bring integration. Vices must be eliminated so that virtue may prevail. The virtues needed are the exact opposite of the vices one has. Once the vices (deterrence) have been eradicated by acquiring their antidotes (virtues), our unique qualities are able to shine forth, and we have become perfect. Although we must eliminate the deterrence which inhibits us, the effort is not to become all in all, but rather uniquely perfect in a specific way. Each person must learn to be true to himself or herself, because no one else can possibly express perfection in exactly the same way as he or she can. The way to arrive finally at the perfect state of being is to be true to our own heart feelings, recognize our faults, and work to eliminate them. Through this effort we see that construction is the basis for all development, and development is our motivating force.

We know, of course, that we all have a long way to go before this state can exist for us. But the knowledge that we are on the right track should be sufficient impetus for us now. Success is made up of moment-to-moment decisions from day to day. Each such constructive effort adds up to the result we seek. That perfection is aeons away is of no concern since we have eternity in which to reach it. What we should work on during each incarnation is not the development of our unique qualities, but rather the development of antidotes to the deterrent elements, our virtues. Little by little, through their acquisition, the unique quality of our being, our contribution to God's dream, becomes evident. Perfection is the total elimination of deterrence.

Reincarnation is God's plan, but can everyone who wants to reincarnate do so?
Problems can develop out of declining birth rate in some areas and increasing birth rate in others, creating an imbalance. Race is a factor too. Race influences environment, and variety in this area is important to give balance to the possible needs.

Can't someone take a hand at adjusting things?
No, for the plan of reincarnation has been set from its inception and will continue until everything works itself

out. Time is the factor here. What seems wrong is merely incomplete. Perfection is the complete elimination of deterrence. Our unique, innate qualities are in themselves perfect.

Is there nothing more to be learned after the elimination of deterrence?

Yes, certainly there is. But this is done in the higher realms where all who reside are in themselves perfect. God's dream is to be augmented endlessly, and it behooves us to strive to augment our own capacities as fully as possible. After the fundamental state of perfection has been reached, we are through with the reincarnational cycle and proceed to the realms where we work to rarefy our condition and become more and more dazzling to behold. This augmentation is one of intensity, not size. Each stage brings us to a more rarefied atmosphere.

In choosing our parents, do we also know what the circumstances of our lives will be?

No, we don't actually know the various circumstances of our lives. In this matter of free will there is always a protective element. We do have free will to pick our parents for an incarnation, but we don't know at that time exactly how the circumstances will develop. We do know that these parents offer, by their nature, the very circumstances which we think we need. Now here is the crucial point. I said "circumstances which we *think* we need." If our thinking is clear and truthful, all is well and everything goes according to plan. If not, the parents we choose may not create the circumstances necessary to coincide with the plan. In this case, the plan will be altered to result in the most constructive outcome. I have said that the circumstances developing from our decisions alter the events of our lives. This is true in the

Place of Preparation too. If we create the wrong circumstances (parents), the events which result alter the master plan.

*Are you saying that the ideal parents exist and it is
our job to find them each time?*

Yes. There is one set of ideal parents for each incarnation. If we see our needs clearly, we will find them. If not,
our choice will contribute something different but constructive at the core, and the plan will be adjusted to
include the circumstances which develop. There are
many elements which go into the master plan. Our own
desires and needs are one element; the ultimate objective is another; and the relationships we need to develop
are still another.

This is a social universe. We all have important relationships which contribute not only to our ultimate
goals but also to each incarnational link to those goals.
Everyone who is involved makes his or her own unique
contribution to the overall plan of an individual life.
The master plan which results from all of these factors is
reconsidered each time an incarnation is anticipated
and adjusted according to need. The plan is com-
puterized, so to speak, and out of the computer comes
the plan of each incarnation. We who are taking this trip
do not know much of the plan, except for what we ourselves have put into the computer. The rest is the result
of all the other factors.

*How do we come to experience being male or female,
father or mother, sister or brother, and so on?*

By choosing our parents, we choose all the rest too. The
circumstances which develop from this choice determine these factors. This is why the important decision is choice of parents. We choose our parents according to our opinion of our needs. If we see clearly at this

point, our needs will be met. If not, our real needs and the circumstances which develop may prove at odds with one another. This can be remedied, however, by choices made during an incarnation.

If we make the original mistake, how can we be expected to make the right decisions thereafter?

We can't. We must work things out as we see them. We are responsible for the outcome of an incarnation, and we may very well learn from our mistakes. If we don't, we will continue to have them because the circumstances we set up call for them. By reacting constructively, however, we can alter subsequent events and change the circumstances of our lives. We are drawn into continuing relationships for a variety of reasons. The most important reason is love. Love expresses itself in many ways, and it is logical to want to continue a relationship in one way or another through many incarnations. This doesn't necessarily go on forever, but a strong relationship can work itself out in many, many ways through a long series of incarnations. The incarnational cycle is short compared with the time we spend in the Place of Preparation, where we have plenty of time to consider parents and relationships. Even though we can make mistakes in regard to our parents, we will always be where we should be in a given incarnation, because no matter how faulty our thinking has been about our true needs and the choices we have made concerning them, the circumstances which develop are the result of our decisions. Any set of circumstances can develop for good because beneath all events lies construction and the opportunity to build. Such an incarnation may not be in line with the plan, but it is a rare incarnation which is perfect, and the opportunity to correct and rebuild is always present.

Everything you need is provided for you from this

side. The source of all your needs and desires lies here. On earth you have an opportunity to work out problems you have given yourselves, but the assistance comes from here. Our lives are all planned out in advance here, and then we either follow the plan or deviate from it, depending upon our understanding. This makes it sound as though we have no real choice in our own growth, but we do. In saying our lives are all planned out, I mean that the ultimate objective for an incarnation is decided upon and the various possible routes to it are outlined. Which of the routes we follow is our prerogative, but progress toward our goal is essential. If we react productively to events, we will indeed be living by one of the many possibilities.

Don't ever worry about being sidetracked indefinitely. There is always a favorable way out of every dilemma. A great blessing provided by God is this constructive possibility innate in all events, the grace of God. *By God's grace all deterrence can be turned to good.* It is through our mistakes that we learn. Things are not what they seem, and with the desire for truth, we can always find the value in every event.

All assistance comes from this side. Even the ability to see clearly and recognize right from wrong involves the use of spiritual equipment—love, sense of truth, and intuition, all of which have been acquired on this side. So you see how important it is to keep in communication with this side. It is possible for everyone through prayer and mental projection. For some it is possible in more involved ways, but everyone has some way to bring himself closer to the source of his life and all of life. The act of communication helps to open channels to love and construction and let them flow through us and help us in ways we don't realize consciously, but which we can come to recognize intuitively.

When we choose the right parents, we control our lives

from the beginning. It is we who have decided we were ready to move on, and it is we who have decided just what problems were to be solved this time, and it is we who have chosen the parents who would provide us with circumstances most conducive to success. We did decide to be born again, and we did provide the circumstances in which we live. Since this is the case, we had better get to know ourselves. The situation is our responsibility, so the solutions to our problems can be found within our own capacities. Our spiritual equipment can help us solve all problems. Knowing ourselves is the answer. By being obedient to our heart feelings, we are obedient to God. This is our responsibility. The qualities that are acquired on this side are many, including humility, faith, hope, charity, energy (yes, energy is a most important constructive element), patience, clarity of vision, loyalty, and others. Although our spiritual equipment has been there from the beginning, it can always be sharpened before reentering each time.

Just how these qualities are acquired is complicated to explain. But I can say it is through instruction and guidance by those who are the teachers of truth. The process is one of realization by suggestion, and not one of setting down rules to be learned. Learning is conceptual and cannot become permanent until it is lived out on earth. Here we are growing and nurturing the tree, and there you use it to build your house in spite of all the problems which beset you in the process. You are attempting to build your house in the wilderness, and persistence will enable you to achieve your goal, in spite of theft, storm, fire, and hurricane, which threaten to overcome you. If you build your house securely on the rock of faith, you have nothing to fear.

By this time I had begun to wonder how all this preparation was carried out on earth. Since each lifetime is
planned out, I was concerned about how the plan
worked itself out in the process of living.

*When you say each life is planned out, do you mean
that the span of it is predetermined?*
When we reincarnate, the plan of our lives includes the
span of our lives. Remember that our main concern is
results. Time spent on earth must be profitable. The
reason for reincarnating at all is to achieve qualities
needed for development. If we think our lives should be
spent in the pursuit of pleasure only, we are in for some
surprises. A predetermined length of time is given in
which to get specific results. Usually that time is lived
out more or less as planned. How it is lived out is up to
us. The quality of life is our responsibility. All events are
purposeful, and if we gain from them we will progress,
no matter how they affect us physically. We are living by
the grace of God, but the quality of our lives depends on
us.

There are two situations which can alter the span of a
life. First, if we are not living up to our potential, or if we
violate our achievements appreciably, we may be re-
called before the span of our life is up so that we won't
inhibit our progress too much. Second, if we are making
more advanced strides than anticipated, we may be
allowed to live out a longer span in order to take advantage of the circumstances we have developed. Many who
die young have satisfied the need for that incarnation
and must move on.

The goals of the plan are always adhered to, no matter
how many detours and roadblocks occur along the way.

To understand ourselves and our relationship to the rest of things is to understand how to progress according to plan. When we understand that everyone has an opportunity to realize good from every circumstance and event, we know that God's love permeates and God's will dictates all. We have only to obey the rules.

I realize that once we are here on earth, we find ourselves in the environment which is part of the circumstances of our development. These circumstances must influence our development greatly. Could you please expand on this subject?

We are now discussing the primary influence of an incarnation. The circumstances of our lives all generate from our initial decision, the choice of parents. Our parents provide us with our environment, our physical characteristics, our sex, our intelligence, our talents, our station in life, and our personality. These circumstances of our lives contribute all that we need for our spiritual development. And since development is the purpose of an incarnation, you can readily see the importance of these circumstances. Once we find ourselves here with the parents of our choice, there is no turning back; the die is cast. We have a responsibility to live out this life to the best of our ability in accordance with our prior decisions. We influence these circumstances, of course, by our reactions to the events which develop and our decisions concerning the subsequent circumstances. If our reactions and decisions are constructive, we are benefiting our lives. If not, we are deterring our development. Follow your heart when making decisions, and you will always be reacting constructively and living according to God's will.

Heart Feelings

Follow my heart! Was that essential to making constructive decisions? Could anything as fickle as whims of the heart be important to spiritual development?

Will you please clarify the instruction "Follow your heart"?

Our hearts are the centers of our beings. We must keep ourselves close to those feelings and allow them to influence our thoughts and actions. If we exercise faith in every possible way, pray in earnest, and envision all of the situations and conditions our hearts dictate, constructive future events will result. The more we live in accordance with our heart's wishes, the more our future will develop according to God's will. Our lives have been planned; all we need to do is consult our hearts for the plan. Whatever we *really want* is what has been planned. Our tomorrows are assured if our todays are lived according to the dictates of our hearts. We really do have the answers to all of our problems, because the answers lie in the heart. It is the only source of information which has value to us. Our job is to uncover the source by examining our feelings. Our heart desires what is right for us, our purpose, and our potential. We have specific goals to accomplish and the means through which to accomplish them. Allow your heart to reign and your imagination to take over. Out of this free imagining from the heart you will come to see quite clearly what your true path and goals are. The answer to "Who am I?" and "Why am I here?" can be found by following your intuitive feelings, which stem from your heart. Intuition is a prompting of heart feelings, which are your ties to your source. Heart feelings lie at the core of our being and can only be discovered through self-examination; what we *really* want as opposed to what we think we want, or what our compulsions demand or outside pressures suggests. These heart feelings stem from the needs and desires of our eternal being, and they point the way toward our spiritual objective this time. Also from the heart comes the sense of truth and feelings of love, your spiritual equipment. The source, then, of all you need is your heart, and your heart feelings must be cherished and nourished. Dreams are intended to inform in descriptive ways what the spirit wants. Your spiritual mind is your intuition, and this lies in your heart, not your head. Many people are unable to relate to God or reincarnation or any matters of a spiritual nature. But for everyone, "What do I really want?" can be answered. By getting down to this basic question, we are able to see more clearly and to understand the constructive nature of our hearts' desires. Once this realization has penetrated, we are freed to explore the nature of construction (God's will) and indirectly learn about God and our relationship to Him.

Try not to depend upon the advice of others, because the answers for you lie within you, lodged in your heart. By bringing your true feelings to the surface, you find the answers to your questions. So it is with everyone. The problem is, so many people are unwilling and therefore think themselves unable to dig deeply enough to find the pay dirt. They would rather follow someone else's advice than spend their energy and concentration on themselves. The only person who really knows you is *you*. We must never lose faith in ourselves, because we are individuals and therefore special in the eyes of God. Our goal is union with Him. Inner feelings emanate from the spirit's needs and wishes; they are our connection to our eternal being, the desires of the God in us. Our spiritual equipment belongs to our spiritual being. By using our spiritual equipment to satisfy our heart feelings, we are clued in to spiritual achievement.

When I say that we come prepared to cope with earth life, I mean that there is a purpose in our being here, and the clues to that purpose and the means for achieving it are to be found in our heart feelings. We are here because we want to be here, and the job we have to do here will advance us spiritually. If you follow the path which your heart says you are capable of traveling, you will be led, through this effort, to the endeavor which will bring you the growth factors you need. If your capabilities don't seem to relate to what your heart feelings want, they will, if properly utilized, lead you in the right direction. The way we think and act will create the kinds of circumstances which will influence the events of the future. Construction is God's will, and the constructive effort will always lead us to God's will, our spirits' needs and desires, our true heart feelings.

Trust your feelings. Don't be afraid to look at them closely and savor them. Once you have been able to dig deeply enough, cherish what you discover, because you have found the answers to your problems. Nothing that happens to you is as important as what you think about it. Never was this statement more meaningful than at the moment of self-discovery. The satisfaction of the desires and needs you have uncovered will surely point

the way toward your ultimate goal and will make this
incarnation a successful one.

How can I be sure that what I think I want is my heart's wish?

Your spiritual equipment will never lead you astray. You
can always trust it to guide you. The concern which
most people have with their lives has to do with getting
ahead, being successful, making money, having the
amenities of life. The problem with this kind of thinking
is that it is backward. If we search our hearts to expose
our innermost desires and dreams to the light of understanding, we can learn more there that can affect our
future than anywhere else. In your heart lies all you need
to learn in order to develop into the kind of person you
want to be. We are, of course, talking about spiritual
development. Fame and fortune can become hollow,
temporary situations in a life destined for spiritual perfection. To separate what we really want from what we
think we want or what our emotions compel us to do is a
difficult task. But once achieved, it can result in real
growth of the spirit. The circumstances of our lives are a
boon to us, and we must learn to recognize their real
value, no matter what they appear to be. We get what we
need. We need what we get. Construction lies at the
heart of all events. Harmony and construction are the
true exponents of love and will. They are found in the
heart feelings.

Aren't my emotions the same as my feelings?

They are feelings, of course, but not your deepest heart
feelings. It is necessary to clear away the upsetting emotions and our reactions to the emotions before we can
look deeply enough to uncover our real feelings. These

feelings are often misplaced by emotions, and it is necessary to understand the difference.

To find what you really feel about something takes
time and a willingness to throw off all attachments,
such as emotionalism and compulsion. Whenever you
are hit be a wave of emotion, allow it to pass through
you, shake yourself free from it, and examine the situation from your heart. This effort will eliminate a great
deal of the deterrence which results from giving in to an
emotional reaction. Such emotionalism is self-serving
and has nothing to do with your true feelings, the eternal you. Emotions tend to throw up a smoke screen,
which makes it impossible to see. Step aside from this
turmoil and allow the smoke to settle before you try to
examine your real feelings. In this way you can avoid
confusion and find the answers to your problems. Study
the procedure to understand it fully.

If we are trying to live God's will for us and are not sure
just what we should be doing, we can always find out by
getting closer to ourselves and consulting our inner
feelings. Lying deeply within us is the knowledge of what
is right for us and how to go about getting it. We must
open up to ourselves by bringing our concentration
down to the simplicity of true heart feelings. We must be
willing to look inside to discover who we are and what to
do with our lives. The thought process is very beneficial
in helping us to recognize the truth. Think of what
would be the most wonderful situation in the world to
you, not superficially but deeply. What are your real
desires, your real needs, the circumstances you can't
imagine could ever occur? As you are thinking these
things through, you are giving them reality, bringing
your life's plan to the surface, reinforcing its energy, and
giving it reality. The plan is always activated to combat

deterrence, but it is more fully activated by the force of our own constructive thought.

Thoughts are things, and these things spark a fuller and more complete set of circumstances, which, in turn, spark constructive events. By our thoughts we can expedite progress and development. Nothing can defeat the ultimate purpose, but much can deter it. Our thoughts motivate our actions, one way or another. There is no way to end our lives; we are willed to live forever. We can, however, deter our development. It is through our thoughts that we either help or hinder the plan of our lives since we can never get away from ourselves. We must recognize our true relationship to our Maker and become a part of the plan by functioning constructively. If we search our hearts with every issue that comes along, we will eventually be able to see the difference between what we want and what we do. We will learn that even though we understand what our hearts want, we are seldom able to achieve it. The reason is that the very thing our hearts want is often the opposite of what our compulsions dictate. The internal struggle is the most important aspect of our earth life. If we are prepared and persistent, we will find that our will, as expressed by desire of the heart, can cope with the difficulties.

Remember, the energy of deterrence fades; if we just hold on, it must give in. To lose the battle of the day is not very important in the long haul if we don't lose heart in the process. We must recognize that at every level it's a battle, but the more we consult our hearts, the more we understand and are able to cope. Those of us with the greatest struggle have the most to gain or lose. The effort is always worth what it costs, since without it we would never be able to reach our goals. We are all in this together, and we can help each other, but the crux of each problem is ours to solve. We come to this battleground expecting to win. But the need is for energy and desire, both of which are ours to generate. When we fail, we are failing ourselves, and in doing this we are failing our fellow beings and our Father as well. The more we are responsible to ourselves, the more we are responsible to God.

Self-Examination

Richard had mentioned self-examination in relation to uncovering heart feelings and learning how to cope with life.

How do we examine ourselves?

Human beings have been provided with a key for understanding what is constructive for them: their heart feelings. Therein lies the God element, the still, small voice, the sense of truth. Consulting our heart feelings, which always lie hidden, often takes much probing and the recognition and separation of true feelings from compulsions. The result comes with effort. What do I really want? How do I really feel about this situation? What is the most beneficial thing for me to do? If I could dream it up, what would it be? Probing in this way, we come closer to the eternal being and the reasons for being where we are. The circumstances of our lives, our abilities and talents, our interests and our heart feelings, are all part of our spiritual background designed to help us understand ourselves, why we are where we are, and what we are to do. In order to learn about ourselves, we must first open up for inspection. Search your heart for your deepest feelings and reactions, and examine them. Let the conditions of your life go from your mind; forget your unhappiness for the time being.

If we turn our backs on all negative thought and search our hearts, what do we find? Do we find desires, hopes, and expectations? If so, we are looking at the framework for a possible outcome of our lives. When we feel that these dreams go way beyond the realms of possibility, we try to shut them out. But wait a moment. Instead, examine them carefully; try to imagine what must go into their realization. Then look at the circumstances of your life. Is there any way they can be of use in furthering your heart's desires and dreams? Before you proceed, you must ask yourself whether these dreams are important enough for you to make the effort to achieve them. If your answer is yes, you are on your way toward understanding yourself better.

Now, we must all grasp one fact clearly. The circumstances of our lives are designed to help us acquire those elements best suited to our development. Our true desires lead us to our purpose, and the circumstances of our lives will make that purpose possible. We are guided by our spiritual equipment (love, sense of truth, and intuition). When we apply them to our situation, a possible path will begin to open up in our minds. By pursuing this path, we may find our lives unfolding in unexpected ways or heading in directions we hadn't before considered. But we can be assured we are on our way toward development. We may find that our goal this time doesn't become apparent for some time to come, as each new development builds on the others in a constructive way (according to God's will). We must find the truth which lies hidden in all events.

The truth can be found in our own heart feelings, but how do we learn about them? The way is not difficult, but it demands complete honesty. If we are to find the truth, we must be willing and able to look into our hearts. We can use our reactions to the events of our lives as a basis for evaluating our progress. If we think the initial reaction to an event is the right one, we are only looking through our emotions, which are misleading because by their nature they are self-protective. This reaction to an event can only hide the truth still more deeply, unless we are capable of separating our real feelings from our emotions. This is the first step, to ignore all emotional reaction. The next step is to collect ourselves and search for an answer. How do I really feel about this situation? In what way is it beneficial to me? How can I best profit from the event? How does it really affect me? What do I need to learn? What lesson is being taught here? By accepting the event and clearing away our emotions, we learn from the answers to our questions.

Keep in mind the fact that there are no accidents, that events are the results of the circumstances which produced them, and you will be able to see things more clearly. Every event has a purpose, and our job is to see the purpose behind it. Clear vision comes from a pure and humble heart, devoid of emotionalism and compulsion, and open to truth. The only way to evolve properly is to react to the events of our lives constructively. If we wait until we see a path developing, energy flowing in a specific direction, we can, by aligning ourselves with this energy, learn where we are being led. Don't start anything unless you have a clear understanding that it is a reaction to existing circumstances. Events are the result of circumstances, and we must make sure that we don't contribute to circumstances which bring in events of a deterrent nature, by our abortive efforts to make things happen. These results must be overcome before we can get back on the right path.

In looking for the occupation which will further our development, do we all have options, whether or not we recognize them?

The options in life are few. They depend upon the circumstances and talents we have been given. It isn't possible for most people to pick and choose what they will do from among many possibilities. Most of us have the ability to do one or two things well, and these become the clues to our purpose. Opportunities are not very prevalent, and most people are content with a single occupation. For those few who must make a choice from among the many talents with which they have been endowed, the decision can be complicated but necessary since there is always one direction which would prove the most beneficial. The great souls who can do many things with equal benefit are rare. The person who knows what he wants to do and what he can do is the enlightened one. We must recognize that we all have a purpose and that the purpose is related to our abilities. Having too many abilities offers a problem.

Most of us haven't grasped the fact that we are where we are of our own volition and that there is a reason and purpose for being where we are. The only way to understand this is to examine ourselves, using our abilities. Everyone has the ability to search his heart for his true feelings. These feelings enable us to see that we have desires and wishes and that we also have abilities. In sorting this out, we learn that our needs and our equipment can meet on common ground. Then we ask ourselves why we have these particular needs and this particular equipment. Is it just an accident? Does it have a long-range purpose? What is the point of striving to better myself? Can it be that the charlatans and crooks are smarter after all? The answer to these questions, if they truly come from the heart, will lead to the realization that there is a strong pull in the direction of construction and that this pull must be more than happenstance. The urge for survival and the urge to evolve are closely related and fundamental to our nature. There must be a reason. Reincarnation suddenly shows itself as the logical answer. We have come with a purpose. Our desires and talents can be clues to that purpose, and our spiritual equipment helps us find it. The person who has been given many abilities and many interests must, of course, learn to sort them out and come to an understanding about his needs.

What interests us and what we need are not necessarily compatible. We may often be interested in things which merely exaggerate our problems. There are many compulsive interests which people exercise that in themselves are merely manifestations of basic problems. An example is your need for concentration, which this work has forced you to accept. You know now that your quick and alert mind contributed to your inability to settle down to concentrated effort. And as long as you were giving in to your ability to grasp things quickly and your compulsive need to be aware of everything around you at once, you were keeping yourself from developing concentration.

The growth factor in making a choice and following it through is enormous. The conditions of a life are designed to bring out the best in a person's nature and to develop qualities sorely needed. As everyone's needs are individual, so the circumstances of each life are individual. Each one's abilities are uniquely related to the circumstances of each life. We can function within the circumstances of our lives, and our intent has been to develop. This is true no matter how it appears to be on the surface. Being honest with ourselves is essential to self-knowledge. Until we can accept ourselves as we are, with all our imperfections (the reason why we are here), we won't be able to move forward according to the plan. If we accept the fact that our present experience is intended for our development, then we are open to consider that it is part of a larger plan for our lives. The ability to make choices is a God-given right and a function of God's grace.

How do you reconcile the idea that we have few options with your advice to "dream it up"?

When I say, "Dream it up," I mean that you should try to imagine what you would like most to do, to be, to become. For most people this is a limited experience. They can imagine one or two things, and nothing else has any reality for them. For those who are able to dream up many possibilities (however wild or fantastic), the options become far greater. However, you must try to "dream it up" for yourself in order to make sure that what you do is what *you* want to do.

Who am I?

"Who am I?" is a difficult question to answer. Scientific explanations attempt to answer "Who are *we*?," not "Who am *I*?" Most people have a sense of their individuality, but that's as far as it goes. Consider the fact that there are no two snowflakes exactly alike. We take our individuality for granted without realizing what it means. We are individuals, and our wants and needs are individual, so that makes each of us unique.

Most people believe that man evolved from lower forms of life. But man has remained man for a very long time. Are we at the end of evolution? Is there a further evolvement to be expected? Doesn't science tell us that the universe is continually evolving? Is man evolving in some way we are not aware of? Is there more to man than meets the eye? Could our present evolvement be spiritual? Are we here for a purpose? Do we indeed live forever? Is there Mind behind the orderliness of the universe? If so, how do I relate to that? These are questions for which you must find the answers before you can understand who you are.

Are we helped to find our way in other ways besides through our talents and abilities?

Dissatisfaction for no apparent reason, unhappiness, insomnia, illness—all are indications that our inner being is trying to tell us something. Our lives may not be following the plan which was determined by our choice of parents, the plan which the circumstances of our lives were to develop. Somewhere along the line we may have made the wrong decisions, which created circumstances not to our best advantage. The plan of our lives is one of intent. The circumstances of our lives create events which bring about subsequent circumstances and events, all of which should contribute to our growth. Our own input must be constructive if the plan is to be realized. The way we react to events is crucial to the development of the subsequent circumstances. If we react emotionally out of compulsion or negativism, if we fail to see the construction which lies at the base, then we are altering the conditions of our lives and deviating from our goal. This brings about inner dissatisfaction. This inner unrest manifests itself in many ways, and the problems which develop can be solved only through self-examination, understanding our heart feelings, and acting upon them. We know ourselves better than anyone else does, and we can best discover the roots of our own problems by understanding and accepting our heart feelings, our daydreams, our night dreams, our hunches as part and parcel of the needs of our spirits. Imagination is the closest link we have to the world of the spirit, and through it is found understanding. Our own way of doing things is best for us, but our compulsions are not our true feelings. We must be willing to

examine our true feelings and trust them. Trust yourself
to act constructively. If you hadn't thought you could,
you wouldn't have decided to reincarnate. The eternal
you, who is found in your heart, knows what your wants
and needs are.

The most important function of a lifetime is self-
examination. It must be a continuing activity as regular
as brushing your teeth. The reason is obvious. As we
develop through the application of understanding, our
needs and desires change, if not necessarily in kind, at
least in quality and value. It then becomes necessary to
adjust immediate goals to line up with our altered
growth needs. Regular self-examination is necessary to
clarify our needs and goals. Even as we have long-range
and individual goals which relate to them, we also have,
within each incarnation, goals which change and develop as we achieve them. Keep up with your progress to
know yourself better with each examination. Events,
too, often bring about changes in our personality, stemming from our reactions to events, which bring to light
new facets to our being to be understood and handled
constructively. Through the constant application of
self-examination, we understand the need to grow and
develop and how this is accomplished. We also recognize
that we are right where we should be, and we are glad to
be there, progressing according to the plan. We thank
God for His love, which has made all of this possible.

Can we be aware of our faults without self-examination?

Try to remember just when you learned about your
faults. Did you recognize them before you sought them
out with my help? You had a vague notion but were
wrong about the source of your problems. You had never
sat down and tried to analyze your faults. You think if it

hadn't been for me you would still be floundering. This is an example of just how long we can live in ignorance of ourselves, unless we are willing to try self-examination in the cold light of day with utmost honesty.

Often, when people do recognize their faults, they don't see themselves in relation to an overall plan of life. They hate themselves for their faults because they feel victimized and helpless and blame their parents for their problems. The fact that the faults can and must be overcome is very hard to accept under the circumstances. Therefore, it is only by recognizing who we really are and how important we are to God's dream that we can put our faults in proper perspective. When we realize that we are worthy of all the effort we can possibly make on our own behalf and that we do have the equipment to solve our problems, we find the necessary energy and desire to get on with it.

In examining ourselves, we must first recognize that everyone on earth has faults or they wouldn't be where they are. Particular faults show up in day-to-day encounters and in emotionalism. Recognizing that emotionalism is an outward manifestation of an inner fault, you must search for the cause. Since most problems fall into categories, you will likely find yours among the many recognizable sins: pride, vanity, lust, anger, covetousness, sloth, envy, gluttony, insecurity, lack of faith, fear, hate, and so on. Pride, which is the essence of self-will, is the antithesis of God's will and the fundamental fault of mankind. All other faults are secondary to this.

If we believe our faults are irredeemable, we are giving ourselves a really hard time of it. The need to understand and act upon our faults is so crucial that the very circumstances of our lives are designed to assist us in this effort. The subsequent events and altered circumstances which develop in the course of a life are there to teach us the lessons we need to learn. If we don't respond to events constructively, we will continue to have circumstances that will drive the points home. Progress is the name of the game, and all the rules are regulated to achieve it. Both acting to rid ourselves of our faults and pursuing our heart's desires are essential to a successful incarnation. We must, first of all, recognize our faults and want to eliminate them, and then we must recognize our inner desires and talents and want to develop and fulfill them. One side helps the other, and the result is success. Even if we don't complete the job, every little effort helps to balance the scale or tip it toward construction. The very faults we need to eliminate can become overpowering when put to the test. It takes a well-prepared person to handle them and know that he or she has come to do a job. Woe unto the person who chooses to reincarnate unprepared! The decision is ours, but we must be up to it. Otherwise we will end up in arrears. This is the battleground and we had better come prepared to fight the good fight *with ourselves*!

How do we learn about our faults?

Sit down and examine your feelings. What traits are distasteful to you? How do you act and react with your loved ones, your friends, your colleagues, your boss? Do you have feelings of envy, hate, fear? Are you a bully? Do you measure up to what you expect from yourself or from others? If not, in what ways do you fall short? What in your personality do you think needs changing? Are you simple and honest and truthful with others, or do you hide behind a facade? Are you deceitful or cautious? We don't need to be left guessing about anything; we have the answers. We must not let the surface of things affect our thinking. Things are not what they seem. The truth lies hidden. The inner voice is the voice of the "you" who wants so much from this experience that he is willing to trust in the newly acquired qualities to cope with his problems. This "you" sees clearly and can advise on all matters. You are your own best friend. You will be put right by the inner voice.

Where does conscience fit into this picture?

Conscience is another matter entirely. There are two of us occupying our bodies, the alpha body (the one we see) and the beta body (the one we don't see). Our conscience is the reaction of our minds to the circumstances of life as they have been developed. It is a function of the alpha body and a secondary guide to behavior. However, we must understand that right and wrong are fundamentally individual matters. What is right for you may not be right for someone else. What is right at one time in life can be wrong at another. If you think something is wrong, it is wrong for you, no matter what anyone else thinks. Likewise, if you don't think something is wrong, it isn't, no matter how society may judge you. When we do something we know is wrong, our conscience will so remind us. The inner voice is the voice of the beta body, available to all because each of us is two

The inner voice plus spiritual equipment are the tools of spiritual progress during an incarnation. We come prepared. The only way to know our problems and solve them is to know ourselves. The only way to know ourselves is to trust ourselves and our feelings, to recognize our uniqueness and accept that because of it, we are the only ones who can really know ourselves. Our dreams are not foolishness. They are expressions of our inner being. It is imperative to get acquainted with the eternal being. Compulsions are part of feelings too. They are manifestations of problems which developed from past decisions. Free will grants us one of two choices, the right one or the wrong one, construction or deterrence. At the moment of decision, all of our energy thrusts itself upon the situation, and we apply it to one side or the other. This adds an ingredient to our being, the ingredient of choice. If the choice is deterrent, we are adding to our karmic problems, all of which must be ultimately eliminated. The need to understand ourselves is the most important need to satisfy. Without this knowledge, we are just floating with the tide and subject to it. Our own currents lie latent within us, waiting to be tapped. Seeking self-knowledge is basic to achieving our ultimate goal. Nothing we accomplish during a lifetime on earth can possibly equal what we gain from understanding ourselves and acting upon that understanding. Our real needs lie in our heart feelings, even though we, let alone others, may find them difficult to accept.

Couldn't this emphasis on self be regarded as an expression of self-will?

It is true that to some it could appear so, but remember that self-knowledge leads to construction. We are trying to understand our true nature, to know our Godlike qualities and be able to grow toward perfection. This is an all-embracing concern not limited to ourselves but rather recognizing our kinship to all of life—God. With this understanding, relationships change. We know that we are all in this together and that we have a common bond with our Father. We need to help each other if we are to move forward. By helping others we help ourselves. There is nothing selfish in self-knowledge. If we are capable of recognizing our problems, we are also capable of solving them. The solution is found within the realization. Our spiritual equipment will not fail us if we put our trust in it. Can you begin to see the importance of faith in yourself and your capabilities, faith in the fact that your presence on earth is purposeful, faith in the knowledge that all problems have solutions and that the solutions lie within you, faith in the Mind Who conceived us all?

The way to come to grips with our problems is to face up to them. The vague feelings of unrest and discontent, the events which seem negative, the difficulties which oppress us, the compulsive urges, the unpaid bills, the difficulties of our personal relationships, the misery in our day-to-day living—all are indications of unsolved problems. The realization that there is something wrong at the core of your lives can be the catalyst which impels action. The action is first mental. Thought preceeds action. We can't do anything constructive about our feelings until we learn what causes them. Look before you leap. Don't get caught in the trap of emotional reaction; this would only bring you back to square one. You must be willing to answer the questions I have given you and all others which come to mind by opening yourself up honestly. Before any of this can succeed, two fundamental truths must be accepted. We must believe we are here because we want to be here, and that we have come prepared to cope with our problems. Coping with our problems through constructive living is the purpose of your side of the reincarnational cycle.

How can one prove to a person who says, "I didn't ask to be born," that this is not so?

Each one of us knows deep down inside that he or she has a job to do. This knowledge lies buried under a great deal of emotion, confusion, and deterrence and must be brought out through self-examination. Although we come prepared to achieve our goals, we also come with unsolved problems which we have carried around for a long time. We must put our attention to construction whenever we feel ourselves being overcome by compulsion and negative emotion. Deterrence cannot win out against construction in the long haul, so if we can hold out, we will gain strength and finally be able to dismiss these negatives as unworthy of our attention. This may take a lifetime to achieve, but think of what it does for our development. It is, after all, what you are on earth for.

The problems which develop are all there for a reason. In an orderly world nothing is accidental. Since every event is meaningful and constructive at the core, we must examine the event, no matter how disastrous it may appear, to find the construction which lies within. Even if we believe we didn't ask to be born, we must take responsibility for ourselves and our actions in order to get on in the world. This implies that there is something about us worthy of responsibility.

Self-esteem is basic to understanding and growth. The feelings of unworthiness which prevail are simply manifestations of karmic problems if seen in the light of knowledge and understanding. We are indeed worthy, or we would not be where we are. The solutions to our problems are found in the opening-up process of self-examination. This allows us to look deep inside ourselves to see who we really are and what our purpose is. Be wary of the ready response to self-examination. This is hardly ever from the eternal being, but rather the working of the mind, the voice of the karmic being. In order to make things come out according to the demands of the ego, the mind is busy solving its problems from a self-willed point of view. God's will can be revealed only after an agonizing search of our heart feelings, ignoring our "head feelings" altogether. Self-satisfaction is not our goal. Self-realization is what we are after. This comes from self-knowledge. It is not a simple or easy task, but it is essential if we are to gain from an incarnation.

Purpose

The idea of purpose was new to me. I asked
for an explanation.

*What is purpose? Isn't living constructively in the
moment sufficient?*
We are here for a specific reason. You are there for a
specific reason. The interrelationships are very important. When our common concerns mesh, we develop a
bond of communication and accomplishment beneficial
to us both. We are all children of God, and to the extent
that we fulfill our intentions, we fulfill our purpose and
recognize our kinship with our Creator. Without purpose we are nothing; we drift into deterrence and become negative, causing havoc with our development
and that of others. The drifters are those with the greatest problems. Even negativism, with its damaging results, can bring us around to understanding, through
the lessons learned, more quickly than a state of no
intent, with its chilling, debilitating effects. There is no
standing still. If we are not moving forward, we are
automatically moving backward.

Why you are where you are is due, in part, to the
situation and circumstances of your biological parents
and, in part, to your own needs and desires. We have
chosen our parents because they offered us the kinds of
circumstances which could make it possible for us to
achieve our purpose. We should consider, then, why we
have a purpose. Where does it originate? Development is

indigenous to life itself. Evolution is an accepted scientific theory. Our concern, however, is for the evolution of the eternal spiritual being. The reason we are all where we are has to do with the needs of our spiritual selves. Our physical selves are temporary. They last a very short time in the total scheme of things, and their only importance is that they provide the eternal spiritual being with an opportunity for development. The reincarnational process continues until the soul no longer has need for this experience and proceeds further into higher areas of development in pursuit of the final goal, the ultimate purpose. Each incarnation has a purpose, which is related to the ultimate purpose. In choosing our parents, we seek those who can promise the maximum opportunity for the growth of the quality or qualities we desire.

You might well ask, if we come prepared to achieve our purpose, why do things seem to work out so badly? Why does so much deterrence exist? The reason is that the acquisition of a quality in the Place of Preparation doesn't give that quality permanence. Take humility, for example. We come to earth with good intentions but with pride intact and humility as a possibility only. Humility is what we have come to achieve, but a veil is drawn over our understanding, and we are required to base all of our thoughts and actions on faith in the goodness of God and His plan for us. We arrive with a big job to do and no conscious knowledge of how to do it. We are required to start each incarnation from scratch and build a life through which we can accomplish our purpose.

Although we have help (our spiritual equipment, our mental capacities, and the response to our prayer), we still have problems to overcome. Often these problems can prove too strong for our purpose to conquer. Fear plays a large part in the failure of an incarnation. Also, you must remember that since the decision to reincarnate is ours, it is possible that the pride we wish to overcome, instead of the humility we want to make permanent, has dictated the decision. Proper preparation is essential to achieving our purpose, which is closely aligned with our being. We are, in effect, our purpose. Each of us is a personality that stems from a greater personality which is the embodiment of our purpose. We must learn to grow in our purpose and become complete so that we can realize the ultimate at some point and become a fully functioning element of the whole. To achieve your purpose this time, you must follow these rules:

1. Try to eliminate fear and worry from your life.
2. Try to complete each day as planned.
3. Never become overwrought about daily events.
4. Spend time each day in meditation and prayer.
5. Care for your body.
6. Do daily tasks with care and precision.
7. Try to love all those with whom you come into contact.
8. Live simply.

It is important to acknowledge that we are where we are for a purpose. Life is no accident. We come prepared to cope with it. Things happen for a reason, and it is valuable to know what the reason is and what is to be learned from the happening. We are never victims of our circumstances. We are only victims of our attitudes toward our circumstances. The circumstances of our lives are elements of growth. Don't ever worry about them; they are always constructive. We must believe in our hearts that they will work themselves out to our benefit. That which appears deterrent is merely incomplete. Things are not what they seem. We must have confidence, courage, faith, energy, and concentration so that we can cope with all these factors. Your own abilities will do the job in the long haul, but I must make you aware of the requirements as clearly as I can.

> The purpose of all events is to teach. The learning process continues ad infinitum. But the real value comes from the realization that there is something constructive in every event. Since our goal is perfection, we've got a lot of living to do. What we must hope for is not to have to repeat ourselves too much. We don't want to have to go over the same territory again and again. Our aim must be to learn, truly learn, so we can get on with the growth process. We are still working on the foundation of our spiritual character. The superstructure is a long way off. We don't want to have to tear down and rebuild that foundation over and over again. The ultimate purpose of life is to augment the glory of God. Our own individual purpose is to become a perfect being in our own right, and at-one with our Father. In this way we will contribute to the glory of God. We all have gone through many changes, but we still have a long way to go, and right now we are trying to cope with our present job. This job of self-realization requires greater confidence and concentration than we have had to experience in the past. It also calls upon all the qualities we have developed and are developing to cope favorably with the events of our lives. The more we understand, the more we become responsible for our own actions and the higher the stakes. Free will dictates this. Recognizing that we have what we need and that we can indeed do what is asked of us will enable us to plow ahead without fear, knowing that we are being helped whenever necessary. The purpose of all experience is development. How we react to the experience influences the circumstances which create subsequent events. Knowing this, we must try our utmost to live in faith and the security of love.

Try to spend time each day reminding yourself that everything is really all right. If you keep your mind on your work, and on helping others in any way possible, you will find problems disappearing, and you will become content. Joy is the expression of true understanding. Be happy, trust, love; security comes from this. We help ourselves by helping others. I think you understand this, but we must not let anything dim the vision. Everything develops according to plan if we don't get in the way. If something doesn't develop as we think it should, either the time is not yet ripe or our vision is faulty. If we are keen in our reactions to events, we will sense the trend of things to come. It is very important, however, not to set our hearts on any one solution to a problem. What transpires is always the right outcome to the circumstances which brought the event about. We need what we get. We get what we need. Accept this fact.

The purpose of individual goals, our purpose in being, our purpose in working together, the purpose of life itself, all stem from God's purpose when He created life. Purpose is a means to an end, and the ultimate purpose is perfection. There is no way that anyone can understand himself unless he understands that he has a purpose in being. When we understand why everything is as it is and why we are where we are, we will understand our purpose. Keep this in mind: *We are our purpose.* We and our purpose are inseparable. We are also other things beside our purpose. Those are the things we must eliminate in order to reach our goal and fulfill our potential. We are who we are and what we are because we are destined to become as God. The opportunity is always present. It is God's dream that we shall reach this state. Whether it comes sooner or later is up to us. Free will makes it possible to make choices which lead us toward or away from this goal.

Are you saying that all events are culminations of circumstances which are basically constructive, and that if we don't react to events constructively, the subsequent circumstances will bring about events intended to teach us a further needed lesson?

Yes. It seems complicated, but it isn't. The intent of an incarnation is construction. The plan is to achieve a specific result. Every one of our decisions makes a momentary contribution to the goal one way or another, either to help it along or to deter its progress. But since progress is the goal, it is only momentarily deterred by a negative decision, because out of the new set of circumstances which the decision brings about, construction realigns itself toward the goal. The source of this force is the source of life. Life is of itself constructive; God has willed it so. We are discussing you, but you cannot really separate yourself from the rest of things. Everything that happens is interaction between you and the rest of things. You and your circumstances cannot be separated one from the other. You and the rest of things are part of the same substance, particularized, that's true, but the same substance nevertheless. A negative action separates you from construction, and instead of being one with your circumstances you are separate for a time. You alienate yourself from the rest of things by expressing self-will (deterrence) instead of God's will (construction). The constructive reaction, on the other hand, contributes to the plan of your life with affirmation. In this way you are one with the rest of things as well as being individual. There is no separation of purpose.

In the ultimate state, all of us, according to our ultimate individual objectives, will become perfect parts of greater entities, unique in our own right and essential to the perfection of the greater being. These greater beings become the organs of the ever-evolving All in All, supreme Being, God. This is God's dream, and each of us is essential to it. but until we all realize our purpose, the dream cannot be realized. Our inner being understands our purpose, and we must bring this understanding to the surface, strive for our immediate goal, and get on with our purpose. Self-examination is the answer to all of our questions and doubts on this subject.

There is only one way to achieve your purpose: know yourself. Learn what you really want, and you will be taking the necessary steps toward fulfilling your potential. We become humane through the pursuit of purpose. Whatever we accomplish in that pursuit benefits others in a constructive way. The plan of life must be fulfilled. We are all a part of that plan. We must fulfill our purpose this time if we expect to keep moving. There is nothing to it but to do it!

Potential

Richard had mentioned potential in discussing purpose. I wondered how potential differs
from purpose. It seemed important to know.

*Where does our potential originate? How does it con-
tribute to our ability to accomplish our goals?*

The events of our lives contribute to our development in
that each event offers a growth opportunity. Our potential is developed in accordance with the events in our
lives. The capacity to accomplish is a given factor, but
the realization depends upon how we respond to the
events of our lives. The purpose of the earth experience
is to realize potential so that we can react constructively
to the events of our lives and the spirit can continue to
grow. Potential is determined by goals which we set
before we make this journey. It is, then, the latent capacity to reach these goals. It is through developing our
talents and utilizing our abilities that we come to recognize our true goals in life. We are never expected to
accomplish what we are incapable of doing. We need to
garner our abilities and put them to use so that the
latent potential they represent can be realized. The
relationship between ability and goal is often difficult to
understand. It is only by exploring our abilities to the
limit that we can be led to our goals. Potential is the
untried quality of a person, which must be explored fully
before he can find himself. Every incarnation is set up
with goals and tools with which to reach those goals. If

the tools are allowed to lie and rust, the finished product can never be realized. Our potential (our tools) deteriorates unless used. There is no state as sad as that of a man who fails to realize his potential. Our ultimate potential realized is perfection, but along the way we have a potential to realize in each incarnation, which forms a segment of the whole.

Potential embraces the ability not only to gain certain qualities needed to achieve wholeness but also to eliminate deterrence. The very reason you wish to acquire a particular quality is that you are saddled with its full-blown opposite, and the particular quality needed exists only in the realm of potential until it is put to use by experience. We cannot fight our problems head on and win. The only way to eliminate faults is to turn our backs on them and seek the opposite. By gaining humility we eliminate pride; by gaining peace of mind, we eliminate insecurity. Potential is the built-in ability to achieve construction. Latent capabilities lie within our hearts, ready to be discovered and utilized. To do this, we must be willing to open up and be receptive to influences from without and also to probe our inner being through self-examination.

The acorn is a symbol of potential. In the natural state it falls from the tree, puts roots down into the receptive soil, and grows branches and leaves in accordance with the plan of its life. It responds to the circumstances of its life in the only way it knows, constructively. The circumstances into which we are born are like the circumstances of the acorn. We are where we should be, and only by living as completely as possible, by fulfilling all the requirements of a constructive life, can we realize the potential that is ours to achieve. As the acorn strives for its "treeness," so must we strive for our humanness. We must learn to be true to the nature of whatever category we find ourselves in. We realize our potential by accepting the circumstances of our lives as essential and utilizing them in a constructive way. The apple is an example of self-development. An apple comes from an apple tree, which comes from an apple seed—potential realized.

Potential is realized in the moment. By reacting to our present conditions constructively, we bring into play elements within us which are seeds for growth, our potential. If we seek our potential, we find it within. It is said that we can never run away from ourselves. This is true. But it is also true that we should never run away from our environment. Changes in life are right if they come about through our inner development within our environment. If we run away from our environment out of an inability to face up to its demands, we are playing into the hands of deterrence. We will never realize our potential until we have found ourselves and dealt with our problems and needs. They say the grass is always greener in the other fellow's yard, but this wouldn't be so if we persisted in watering and feeding our own lawns. To neglect what we have and envy others for what they have is to beg the issue. The issue at hand is always self-development, and this must generate within us.

Our potential is limitless (our ultimate goal is perfection, remember), and if we are true to the God within, our potential will blossom forth and we will harvest the fruits of our labors. Our own uniqueness must not be overlooked. With all our faults, we are one of a kind, and our potential, when fully realized, will produce a unique atom of God, completely individual and completely at-one with Him. The way to recognize potential is to look to your heart's wishes. By following what you really want in life, you are pursuing your path and realizing your potential. The circumstances of our lives have all been arranged for the sole purpose of helping us realize our potential. Each incarnation has a specific goal to achieve. We have the capacity to realize this goal, or we wouldn't be where we are. By realizing our potential we are achieving this goal. Each incarnation is intended to make its contribution to the ultimate goal. Our ultimate potential realized is perfection, and our ultimate goal is union with God. The seeds of ultimate realization lie within us just as surely as the seeds of the apple tree (ultimate realization) lie within the apple. All of life functions according to the will of God, and each entity contains within it the potential for ultimate realization. The way for all is accepting the will of God and living a constructive life. The way for each must be to live according to the heart's wishes and thereby realize his or her potential uniqueness. We are all incomplete fragments of God, but each of us is unique, and our ultimate potential is the realization of our unique qualities perfected.

The purpose of life is fulfillment. Fulfillment is the realization of potential. Our potential is limitless. Fulfillment is a growing thing and has never-ending possibilities. All of life is evolving toward fulfillment, and fulfillment itself is an evolving condition. The never-ending growth, or becoming, which is part and parcel of life itself, must become a conscious desire on our part so that we can contribute our share to the process. We are all evolving, or becoming, whether we realize it or not, but conscious acknowledgment of this fact accelerates the rate of growth and brings us to greater understanding sooner.

We Need What We Get, and We Get What We Need

> "We need what we get and we get what we need." This struck me as a very unusual statement. It seemed to me that hard times and bad luck are hardly things we need.

Do we always need everything that happens to us?
We get everything we need and we need everything we get to teach us how to live our lives. We are imperfect and carry with us much that must be eliminated in the process of development. Everything that happens is purposeful. There are no accidents. The intent of a life tends to work itself out, and the goal of an incarnation is achievement. The imperfections we carry around are the results of our own doing. Free will implies choice, and choice implies opposition—right or wrong, good or evil, construction or deterrence. Our Father will do what is necessary to help us, and He will never fail us. The circumstances which develop in a life bring about events intended to be helpful. We are born into specific circumstances which exist because of the parents we have chosen. Out of this original set of circumstances, the plan unfolds. We make a contribution to subsequent events by the manner in which we react to events as they occur. If our reaction is negative or deterrent, the subsequent events will reflect this and a conflict will occur. If, for instance, at some point you should acquire some holdings and this acquisition is not in your real best

interest, a conflict develops between these two sets of circumstances. God's will always wins out because God's will will be done. A chain reaction of circumstances and events develops, one set opposing another. The circumstances resulting from your choice of parents and those brought on by your self-interests culminate in a new set of circumstances, involving both constructive and deterrent forces. When this occurs, construction always wins out, bringing with it events to set things straight again. This converging of circumstances causes all change, from major calamities down. The only way to avoid this kind of experience is to keep close to your heart feelings (your source) and react productively to events as they occur.

Every event has a constructive base, and every time something happens which appears unfortunate, we can, through the use of our spiritual equipment, discover the lessons to be learned, the path to follow, the way to surmount any problem, and the constructive solution which leads toward growth and development. We must understand what lies behind events, what causes them, and why they are important. Development, with all that it entails, is the most important factor in life. When we consider development, we must take into account all of the factors which go into it. We were created as sparks of life, minute individual entities for the sole purpose of achieving—through God's will, His love, and our own efforts—Godhood. God wants to augment Himself endlessly, through the development of perfect souls, uniquely individual and uniquely at-one with Him at the same time. The very hairs on our heads are numbered. The physical bodies we inhabit over and over are just means to an end. Through them we give a quality already achieved in essence in the Place of Preparation the quantity needed to become a permanent spiritual factor of our eternal being. Lessons continue to be taught in an effort to get us to see ourselves more clearly.

We are only able to do what we are capable of doing. This seems obvious, but it often follows that we are unhappy because we can't do what others can do, or we can't be what others are, or we can't have what others have. This comes from not looking within. If we don't do or don't have, it's because we don't need. What we have is what we need, and what we need is what we have. This goes for all conditions of life, no matter how sordid or difficult they may appear to be. An alcoholic may need to learn that *he himself* must generate the desire to change by searching his heart before his circumstances will improve. His own sense of worth must become a reality first. Desperation is often the catalyst. We may need to hit bottom before we can shoot back up.

Help is always at hand, no matter how desperate the situation may seem to be, but it requires facing ourselves and listening to our heart feelings. As long as we are willing to delude ourselves into thinking that we are victims of circumstances instead of accepting the fact that we are victimizing ourselves, help cannot be effective. Assess your own unique qualities instead of comparing yourself with others. We are all children of God, and we're all on the same road. We travel in different ways, depending on our needs, but the way for each is his own way, not someone else's. Being true to ourselves and our uniqueness is the only condition required for safe travel.

I find it difficult to relate "You get what you need" to mass killings and the like. Could you explain?
Such matters are beyond our control and have their own unique purpose. Everyone involved is playing a part in a

drama which must reach its conclusion. Once such deterrence is set into motion, it must work itself out before construction can again take over. Just as we recognize that when we, as individuals, give in to deterrence, it seems to have to run its course before it weakens, so it is with mass deterrence. The so-called victims do not suffer in the long run. Even this experience can be beneficial, depending, of course, on how one responds to it.

You are wondering whether such events are planned. They are not a part of the original intent of any life, but circumstances alter events. They occur when crosscurrents of great deterrent strength intersect with the currents of a life plan. At the outset of an incarnation we may realize that such a possibility exists in the environment we have chosen, but, since at that time we are seeing clearly, we realize that being involved in such a situation and reacting constructively could mean a great step forward in our development. *Intent and event do not necessarily result in the same thing.* Events can deter or alter intent, but in the long run, God's will will be done and the good that can come from all experience is a manifestation of the love of God.

Love and Relationships

Richard had said we must rely on our spiritual equipment. I began to wonder how we acquire these elements that seemed so important in battling our problems.

Do we need to develop our spiritual equipment, or do we just have it?

Our spiritual equipment is acquired in the Place of Preparation before we commence the reincarnational cycle. Here we find ourselves as children of the human species. In order to reach adulthood there, we must develop the necessary tools for our development toward ultimate perfection. We go to school to learn our spiritual reading, writing, and arithmetic: love, sense of truth, and intuition. Only after these have been acquired can we commence the reincarnational cycle.

Is the prehuman evolutionary process automatic? If so, how do we arrive at humanness?

You should try to formulate your own ideas and then ask. This question is not relevant here. However, I will say that the evolutionary process is indeed an automatic one up to a point. Animals on the highest level of development often associate with humans and become domesticated. Each experience on the subhuman level has some unique element to offer, so all life experiences the various forms on the way up. The transition takes place in the Place of Preparation.

Do we all have this spiritual equipment to the same degree?

Yes. This has nothing to do with the equipment we are given through our parents for a specific incarnation, such as intellect. We cannot become adult until we have acquired and assimilated our spiritual equipment fully. In fact, we become adult through its acquisition. It must be ours before we enter the reincarnational cycle. If this were not so, God's plan would be doomed to failure. The problems we run into during an incarnation have nothing to do with the lack of spiritual equipment. They have to do with its lack of use.

Are you saying that all people, no matter how they may appear, are capable of the same degree of love, for instance?

Yes. Love is an essential part of our spiritual being which we must acquire before starting the cycle. It is the epitome of human feeling. Recognition, consideration, empathy, sympathy, sharing, understanding, and sacrifice are all manifestations of love. Adoration, desire, and gratification are also parts of the whole, particularized in a specific way. Every manifestation of love stems from the same source, God, and is a minute expression of the all-encompassing love which is beyond our understanding. The initial act of love was the creation of eternal life, and we are the benefactors. By developing our own capabilities, we are contributing to the endless expansion of love and developing a deeper relationship with our Father. We develop the capacity for love through its practice. Relationships are essential to growth, and interaction creates circumstances which can alter events. If we interact with our associates and loved ones in a considerate, charitable, understanding manner, we are creating an atmosphere of love which is both creative and constructive. This doesn't mean the placid acceptance of problems that others thrust upon us. Everyone has his or her own problems to work out, but our response to cries for help should be consideration, sympathy, and construction, never criticism, derision, or judgment. We have an obligation, as creations of God, to act to the best of our abilities as He does, in love.

Try not to be critical of others. Sympathy and construction follow each other automatically. If we feel sorry for someone, we want to help. But we must be sure that what we are doing is beneficial. If our help is requested, it should be kept to advice and consultation. The other person must make the move, not you. Do not do for others what they must do for themselves. This is true in all relationships. Love is not just a show of emotion, but a consideration of the uniqueness of others and their right to try, to fail, and to learn. *A desire for our help expressed by others must be what triggers a reaction from us.* We must never impose our help on others out of our own concern. Such situations are never productive. If someone no longer wants or needs our help, it should be given up gladly, knowing that our responsibility and opportunity are over. Try to avoid the trap of feeling rejected, and you will experience true humility and negate the effects of pride.

Nothing that happens to us is as important as what we think about it. Love is available to all. It is harmony in action, and when I say we must love all with whom we come in contact, I mean simply that we must create the harmony essential to growth and development. This ability comes from the heart and can replace all rancor, dissension, anger, and negative thought. It can create an atmosphere of construction within our sphere of influence and align us with God's will and God's purpose. God's love works through people in both the incarnate and discarnate universes. We must always try to be more sensitive to all of the help which surrounds us. This is essential to the understanding of ourselves and of life and our connection to it. We are all one in God, and we must learn to give and to receive to complete the chain of love which is essential to growth. All of God's concerns for us are prompted and motivated by love. His love permeates all of life. In the Place of Preparation we are able to relate to God's presence more, but those on earth who are pure of heart can see God in all things. It is only spiritual blindness which prevents people from knowing the presence of God and sensing His over-powering love. In the expression of love we are relating most fully to God. The essence of God is love, therefore the essence of all His creation is love. By utilizing our inner feelings, we can come close to understanding God's love for us. When we are true to our heart feelings, we are manifesting God's love for us. As we express love toward others, we are assuring our true place in God's plan and augmenting the glory with our own tiny spark.

The noblest sentiment in life is love. The nature of love is harmony. To live a harmonious life, to seek harmony at every stress point, and to bring harmony into the lives of others are goals which lead to perfection. Striving is basic to life, and love assists us at every turn. The nature of love is the nature of God. The purpose of life is to augment the nature of God. Love is the essential in-gredient which unites us all in God. Act charitably toward others. Rid yourself of judgmental attitudes. Look beneath the facade, and you will discover a child of God. If you should have the privilege of helping in some way, be grateful, because through this effort you will be helping yourself at the same time. Relationships are opportunities, and we must learn to make the most of each one. Relationships are necessary to growth and development. Interaction ignites the spark of divinity in all of us. There is no growth in a vacuum. Our job is to prove ourselves worthy of His love by manifesting Him in all our relationships. To the extent that anyone strives for harmony in relationships, he is working for God and becoming, in his struggle for perfection, like God.

What about sexual love?

In discussing sexual love we must first examine the role of sex itself. The purpose of sex is twofold; to produce offspring so that God's plan can be fulfilled and to experience the ecstasy which contributes to personal fulfillment. Sex is both useful and necessary. It is not the end-all of life, but it is a device for furthering the growth and development of us all. The act at its most developed level provides the ultimate opportunity for two people to share in the ecstasies of God's creation through a loving, giving experience. This is the highest level of constructive effort. However, if used for self-gratification alone, with no love involved, it becomes deterrent.

In dealing with sexual pressures, we must be sure that our own sense of right and wrong is not violated. If two people know in their hearts that what they are doing is not wrong, then for both it is not wrong. If, on the other hand, either one has feelings of guilt, no matter what the partner thinks, it is wrong for that individual. Many people know in their hearts that sexual practices of any kind are not for them. Others feel just the opposite. It is essential to know our heart feelings and follow them in spite of all pressures from without. The only rules anyone should obey are his own rules from his heart.

You might think that following this admonition would lead to anarchy. But I say that anarchy comes from following compulsions, not heart feelings. Our true heart feelings are always right, but we need to find out just what they are. Love brought life into being and sustains the simple forms of life in their development upward. Sexual love is the sine qua non of God's plan. Sex is essential to reproduction, and reproduction is essential to spiritual development. By giving of ourselves in sexual love, we receive not only the love of our partner, but also the love of God, sharing in His gift of ecstasy. By directing our feelings toward our loved one, we are directing our feelings toward God and sharing the act of love with Him. By raising the level and intent of our lovemaking, we are raising the level of our development.

Sexual love is only a part of the evolutionary process and becomes unnecessary when we develop beyond this point. It is important, then, to use it wisely as an instrument of development. The opportunity to engage in sex is ever-present. Since the object of sex is to express love and harvest the fruits of that love, and since we do have free will, we must exercise judgment about the frequency of sexual activity. Sex without love is an unworthy act. Sexual freedom is a symbol of development. In the lower stages of life sex is periodic to satisfy the procreative need. At the human level it is to be experienced with discretion in relation to our love needs and our desire to have children. Sex is a tool of life, not the end-all of life. Those who engage in it indiscriminately are hampering their spiritual development. Discipline and spiritual development go hand in hand whether the discipline concerns weight, physical or mental health, appearance, or sex.

Compulsive sex is not sexual. Whether directed against oneself or another, it is always an aggressive manifestation of another problem. It has little to do with sex, except as a tool of aggression, and nothing to do with love. Love is the motivating force behind all construction. Since construction is the nature of God's will and harmony is the nature of God's love, we can say with certainty that if we, God's creation, live in constructive harmony with each other, we are following His will and thereby developing toward our goal of perfection, God's will realized. To be able to understand our true nature is to recognize all deterrence as unworthy of the gift of life, which has been given in love and which can, through love, develop to perfection. The act of love is in essence an expression of divinity. We must learn the necessary steps in our development toward perfection, but basic to it all is love.

What about love for a friend?

To grow in love we must expose our heart feelings to those with whom we feel compatible. If we feel close to some people for no apparent reason, we are realizing a kindred bond toward a former loved one. Reciprocation of such feelings is a sharing of previous feelings. Each of us returns many times to the same people, but in different relationships each time—some intimate, some casual. It is love which unites us all in the long run and brings us together in different circumstances in each incarnation. You and I are two people who share the same ultimate goal and have known and loved each other through many incarnations and for protracted periods here in between. We are working together now, and before too long we will be together again here. It is the love of God which has united us and brought us together at this point. It is our love for Him and for enlightenment which will enable us to reach our final goal. Allow yourself to open up, expose your heart, and feel close to me as much as possible. Take a chance.

Encourage vulnerability. Don't hide from me or from others. Be receptive. Allow yourself to feel deeply and fully. Don't be afraid to laugh and cry. Keep free from inhibition and fear, and you will find amazing results.

Love can conquer all. It is the love of God which has given us this unbelievable privilege to become like Him. Love is the most important element in human development. At its base is harmony. The nature of God's love is harmony. We know that all real expressions of love have the same nature. The goal of love should be to achieve harmony in all relationships. As a part of our spiritual equipment, it plays an important part in all of our efforts to understand ourselves and the circumstances and events of our lives. Trying to establish harmony in all situations, no matter how chaotic, we are achieving spiritual growth. Coupling harmony with creativity, we are practicing our potential. If love does not create harmony, it is not of God but a selfish expression of pride and vanity and, though it may be disguised, deterrent.

How is love expressed in the spirit world?

Although there is no need for sex in the spiritual world, the possibility of sublime pleasure exists from many sources—sounds, sights, and the tactile pleasure of touch, the most exquisite of which is the fusion of two beings, one with another. This is a form of embrace but much more complete and gratifying. It is the fullest expression of love any two people here can share. The two beings become one, and the fusion is ecstatic. Although this lasts only a few moments, it serves to clarify to those who share the experience a semblance of what the ultimate condition will be, totally individual and totally at-one with God as well. This is the ultimate condition for man. It represents God's dream fulfilled. We as individuals will, at that point, be all that we can possibly be, all that our potential indicates. By fulfilling ourselves in this way we become complete and are prepared to serve the function which was intended for us from the beginning. Since we are creations, this total realization will allow us to become that portion of the total into which our particular design fits. The final result will be our contribution to God's dream.

You are wondering what love has to do with the major internal struggle of life. The answer is love has everything to do with it. Love brought us into being in the first place, and love is making it possible for us to reach perfection. To emulate the love of God is the highest purpose of our lives. If we could possibly react to ourselves and all our relationships in the same manner that our Father reacts toward us, we would have reached success and ultimate perfection. Love is the height of relationships and self-esteem alike. Love is. We are. God is love. We must recognize these facts and act upon them. The quality of love which each of us can become is unique and remains so even in the ultimate state. However, we must remember that love, along with sense of truth and intuition (our spiritual equipment), must be given quantity through use in order to grow. Without use, they remain as potential equipment only and cannot reach their needed goal.

Didn't you say that spiritual equipment was developed as far as it could go before anyone started the reincarnational cycle?

This is correct. But you have overlooked one important element. Nothing gained in the Place of Preparation can become a permanent part of the final product until it has been lived out on earth. We return to the quality/quantity factors. A quality achieved in the Place of Preparation must be given quantity on earth before it becomes permanent. This is the foundation upon which reincarnation is based. Without this need, reincarnation wouldn't exist.

If we come the first time with merely potential equipment for achieving a quality, isn't our situation precarious?

This is correct the very first time. However, from then on, each time we return, our spiritual equipment becomes stronger through use, and the potential desired quality becomes more easily obtainable. The purpose of life is growth, and life must be lived to grow. We must fulfill ourselves to make the picture complete. Interaction is essential to living. Growth requires interaction. People need people. Loving relationships are essential to development. Living a particular situation through constructively in love is the most important action we can take. In the consideration of the entire panorama of God's plan, we must realize that the essential factor is the daily grind. How we react from moment to moment is the answer to the whole scheme of things. Love is the essential to it all.

You say that loving relationships are essential to living. What about casual relationships? Are they important to us too?

We all have a multitude of relationships both there and here which have contributed to our growth and development. Many of the people you feel close to are here in the Place of Preparation now, but they are just as much a part of your life here as they were there. Relationships provide us with the material for building a strong character. Learning to deal with your associates with understanding, tolerance, and love is very strengthening for you. Your family provides you with the love, understanding, and tolerance you need. Your friends are necessary to your growth because through their reactions to you, you come to see yourself more clearly. Their reasons for liking you show you the value of your qualities, and their reasons for disliking you show you the power of your faults. The people who are close to you now have been close to you many times before. The value of these varied relationships is the result of knowing another person in various circumstances. We are brought together each time in a different context. There is much to be learned from varied experiences with the same people. Through these experiences, we develop a special kinship of shared interests, and ultimately, because we all share the same objectives, we become elements of a greater being of like purpose and make our unique contribution to the Ultimate Being, God.

One way we can learn about ourselves is through our family and our close friends. They are people we have known many times over in many different ways. Our association with them brings out in us much that is latent in thought and feeling. Through those with whom we are close, we see ourselves mirrored and we learn more about who we are and of what we are composed. The qualities that we find hard to tolerate in others could be the very qualities our spirits want us to eliminate. If we have compassion toward others for their faults, they are surely not our faults—either we never had them or we have overcome them. To recognize good in others is to understand the good in ourselves. We will all someday be part of a larger body with a common purpose. Until then, we are working to eliminate the faults which would prevent this union. If we feel that most of those to whom we feel close have gone on, we can always find others with whom we feel compatible, since there are many. Be open and receptive and trust your feelings toward others, and you will be rewarded with love. Relationships are essential to growth, and we must see in others and share with others that common bond which holds us together, God's love for us all. You are thinking you feel very emotionally tied to certain members of your family, and you wonder whether or not that indicates closeness of purpose. Your feeling is valid. The family members who mean the most to you are all a part of your future as well as your past, along with the many other people you love.

What constitutes this ultimate state which we will all realize together?

It is composed of unity, individuality, and perfection. This state is the one to which all our spirits are dedicated, whether we are aware of this or not. Ultimate goals are varied, and our close relationships are merely preparations for the unity and harmony which we will share in a common bond of love. Indeed, the way to this ultimate state is through our relationships. We do not exist in a vacuum. The way to atone for our faults is to achieve atonement (at-one-ment), to become at-one with our fellow man and consequently with our Father. This state also includes unique individuality as well as unique at-oneness. Each incarnation involves different facets, which must be lived through so that we can achieve greater understanding and alignment with each other.

". . . As we forgive those who trespass against us" and "It is more blessed to give than to receive" are two examples in Christ's teachings of the importance of relationships. By giving and forgiving we emulate our Father's actions toward us and become more like Him. God acts through people, and if we learn to act and react constructively (according to God's will), we will be able to achieve our goals, both short- and long-term. Love is the most important element in relationships. It is love which makes the difference between success and failure in relationships. Whether it be love of a man for a woman, a parent for a child, a child for a pet, or one friend for another, it is the essential ingredient in relationships. If we believe we are here to do a specific job and we believe that that job is God's will, then we must believe that everything that happens concerning our relationships is intended to further the job in some way. To pray "God's will be done" and mean it is the answer to all questions about circumstances and events. There is no time to give in to envy, fear, or emotionalism of any kind, because we know in our hearts that everything is really all right.

Each encounter we have, no matter how casual, is important. Each contact with another living being is an opportunity. By realizing that all encounters are meaningful, we will keep our hearts open to them and respond to them. What does this mean? It means that we must be open and receptive to another's needs and desires, and we must help to whatever degree we can. However, there will be encounters from which we must disengage ourselves because we are unable to help in any way. Don't try to hold on to relationships that are unproductive. Once construction ends, only deterrence results. There are people with whom we can have a warm relationship for a short period of time, and then our roads separate and we are no longer drawn to them. Let them go like ships in the night, floating silently away to parts unknown and unimportant to us. Take what comes and embrace it. Be grateful for it as long as it contains energy and involvement. If and when that passes, let it go; it is no longer a part of your horizon. Relationships come in and out of our lives for specific reasons and to specific purposes. We must accept them and also be willing to let them go. The continuing relationships we all have make up the framework of the life we expect to share ultimately. They are always with us in one way or another. We reach our goals through our relationships. If we try to fill the present with concentrated loving concern, we will never have to worry about tomorrow. Tomorrow's circumstances result in part from the solutions to today's events.

No event is to be feared, because it comes containing elements of value. When we are able to see this clearly and respond from insight, we will be able to live out a successful incarnation. We fear only what we think will happen. We can always cope with events at the time they occur, especially when we know that every event is an opportunity. Understanding our relationships can also shed light on who we are and why we are where we are. We soon learn just where we are in our development when we examine the manner in which we treat our relationships. The way we react to our husbands, wives, children, or parents clarifies the stage of our development and where our problems lie. The way we treat others is a reflection of the respect we hold for ourselves; if we express hatred toward others, to that degree we hate ourselves. Any expression of feeling toward others is an outcome of the way we feel toward ourselves. If we choose to be charitable toward others, we are, in consequence, charitable toward ourselves. He who respects himself surely respects others and their right to be themselves. We can always measure ourselves by the manner in which we respond to the circumstances of our lives, and the circumstances of our lives always involve others.

Our relationship with our Father is the most intimate

of all relationships. The plan of our lives is our Father's will for us. We have only to live each moment fully and concentratedly and we will be doing all we can to fulfill the plan. We work in His service. The manner in which we relate to others reflects our attitude toward God, our Father. What we have done to the "least of these," we have done to Him. The founders of all the great religions are our personal links with our Father. By living by such teachings, we relate ourselves to God.

The only way to become clear in our minds is to become clear in our hearts. The way we feel about someone is more important than what we think about him. In order to understand our true feelings we need to examine our hearts and find what is buried there. Our relationships hinge upon our heart feelings, not our minds. If we try to develop relationships from a rational standpoint, not only will they be meaningless, but they could also be detrimental. Relationships and love are essential companions. Any relationship which deteriorates into disharmony is no longer constructive and should be dissolved. Divorce is often an emotional resolution to a misjudged relationship. "They whom God hath joined together, let no man put asunder" does not refer to mismarriages, because God didn't join them together with love (they weren't true to their own inner feelings where God dwells). When a church sanctifies a marriage, it doesn't mean that it has been sanctified by God (your inner heart feelings). If we confuse our compulsive, karmic problems with our heart feelings, we can run into great trouble. Don't worry about the children of divorce. Their lot is an opportunity for them to grow too. No situation is of itself wrong. It's what we think and do about it which makes it either constructive or deterrent. Some people have the experience of being married many times and others not at all. Everything depends upon our development needs and how we react to the circumstances of our lives.

Am I right in assuming that family relationships must be of special importance?

Yes. Most family relationships are especially important because they involve us in very personal ways. Since our families constitute our extended beings, so to speak, each incarnation makes it possible for us to blend with members of our families in a different way. When we have various relationships with the same people over and over, we are provided with opportunities to share similar qualities and to rid ourselves of similar faults. Since our ultimate goals are the same, we tend to fall into similar patterns of behavior, and through these associations we can learn to enhance our good qualities and eliminate our faults. Such relationships offer us a mirror in which we can see ourselves. In wanting to help certain members of our families with their problems, we are helping ourselves with our own problems. Inter-relationships within a family offer the necessary give and take of development.

The only concern we should ever have is for another. We solve our own problems by helping others. Our family relationships offer us the greatest opportunity for such development. However, it doesn't follow that every member of our family in any given incarnation shares our ultimate objective. With some we may have only a casual relationship for a specific purpose.

Do the mentally ill benefit from relationships?

Those who suffer from mental illness are those who can no longer cope with their relationships because of their karmic problems. Many people have just as many prob-lems, but because of preparation and previous accomplishment, they are able somehow to deal with their karma and move ahead as well. Still others with as many problems are able to tread water at least. But those of us who want to overcome our problems, but find ourselves overwhelmed by them because of lack of preparation, take one of two courses of action. If we embrace deterrence with an attitude of "If you can't beat 'em, join 'em," we give in to it altogether and become an element of deterrent force. Such an incarnation is wasted and causes a detour in development. A turnabout is possible but improbable. If we continue to try, however feebly, to fight our problems, we are often allowed to step aside so that we will no longer do harm to ourselves spiritually. This condition is referred to as insanity; but at the base it is construction. We are freed from further damage to our growth. Recovery offers an opportunity to try again. As long as we don't truly want to give in to deterrence, we needn't become victims of it. In this way, insanity can be looked upon as a blessing. Mental illness comes about because of unsolved problems that haven't been properly coped with. It is also an opportunity to prevent deterrence from overcoming the spirit by eliminating the function of the will. People with this condition are paying certain debts in this way, but must wait until the next time for any progress.

I can see how the relationship between parents and a mentally retarded child could benefit the parents. How does it benefit the child?
The important element of this kind of situation is the interaction between parent and child. A person who becomes mentally deficient as part of his condition has been given very difficult circumstances to cope with. However, we don't grow spiritually in direct proportion to our mental capacity. A mentally retarded person is

perfectly capable of growing spiritually. To the degree that he grows within the boundaries his condition sets, he is progressing according to plan. Effort achieves development. If such a person makes the effort of which he is capable, he is doing the job. He is often freed of other deterrent problems because of it and is allowed to put all of his energies into learning how to cope with day-to-day living.

The outcome of any incarnation depends upon how we cope with the circumstances of our lives. If we learn through them and live in harmony with our surroundings, we will surely gain from the experience. Those of us who are ready to spend our lives in service to others and know in our hearts that this is our purpose, must learn under what circumstances our efforts will be fruitful. First of all, we must know ourselves and know our capabilities. Once we have developed our talents, we are on our way. Our particular qualities serve as a magnet to draw the proper circumstances to us upon which to act. If service to others is meant to be our job, the conditions favorable to our needs will materialize. Within these circumstances a sphere of influence develops. Within this sphere of influence we are capable of coping with all events constructively. Since the sphere of influence emanates from our talents and capabilities, it is limited in its power to the extent to which they are capable of being effective.

In order to expand successfully, we must understand our limits. The person who wants to alleviate the ills of the world may spend time worrying about the problems of mankind, but he is not being constructive when he does this. His intentions are good, but he is not using his abilities effectively. He forgets that mankind is made up of individuals. If we try to help those individuals within our immediate surroundings, using our talents and abilities, we will be doing everything possible that we can do. Our immediate surroundings include our family, our friends, our neighbors, and our associates. Within this framework our efforts have strength, and growth will result from them. Beyond this sphere of influence, the efforts become diluted and ineffective. There are those who, because of their particular position in life, their particular circumstances, may have a very wide sphere of influence, and what they do may affect many, many people. However, for all of us it is wise to stay within the boundaries of our capabilities, and our efforts will prove effective at any level. Everyone has a sphere of influence within the circumstances of his life. Since relationships are basic to growth, the influence we have on others not only affects them but, more important, affects us and our development. Try always to use the influence you have constructively.

Insecurity

Richard kept stressing that construction is the answer to the problems of living. I wasn't sure I understood how to recognize construction.

How can I always be sure that what I am doing is constructive?

Remember, I have said that everyone has spiritual equipment. Love, sense of truth, and intuition will always direct toward construction. The person who is fraught with insecurity and who has built strong defenses which manifest themselves as envy, greed, fear, pride, and so forth, has been so dishonest with himself that he can no longer see clearly. Such a person would find it difficult to recognize construction. However, the truth is always present, and the same action is required of all. Look at yourself honestly and uncover your true feelings, and you will be taking the first steps toward constructive action. You will recognize that you are very unhappy with yourself basically, but you find it difficult to let go of your defenses. The solution lies within the basic dissatisfaction itself. The usual way to alleviate such problems is to attack the symptoms (not the causes) by turning to drugs, alcohol, and sex in an effort to satiate the basic dissatisfaction and numb the senses.

You have told me that insecurity is one of my basic problems. Please explain this subject further.

Your own importance is related to your own effort. Your value in the cosmic scheme of things depends upon your willingness to recognize who you are and live according to God's will. One primary element in living successfully is truly living in the "now." If we involve ourselves fully in living constructively now, and we realize that now is eternity, we can bring our energy and concentration to now and fill eternity with construction. In this way we are rearranging the cosmic state of things for the better. All of our energy constructively devoted to now leaves no time for indulgence in karmic problems. The most important element in your life now is you and your understanding of truth. The way you live is essential to your work, your health, and your growth in general. It is essential to see the importance of accepting life as it comes and tackling the problems from the pinnacle of faith, hope, and love. There is no problem which cannot be solved, because the solution lies within the problem itself. The solution is built into the situation, but can be discovered only through clear vision. Every circumstance and event of our lives is intended for our growth. When we can see that all is well and that the way out lies in our own responses, we will be able to solve all problems and grow in the process. Be thankful for problems, because we all need them for our development. All problems are there to be solved for our own good. We are the ones who count. Events are not evil. They only become so if the reaction to them is deterrent.

Perhaps you can see now that insecurity comes when we don't live according to God's will, in the moment. Regret is odious, and anticipation is worse. The only time for action is now, so try to keep your mind on the present. When you try this, you will be trying to do what we do here quite naturally. The more you succeed, the more you are with us in spirit. The way to become at-one with the rest of things is to live as they do. All other living things fulfill this requirement by just being. Man must learn to fulfill this requirement by choice, by desire, by will. The choice grants us the opportunity to become like God. Other living things know who they are, and they live their lives according to plan. We are given the opportunity to learn who we are and do the same thing. Other creatures live perfectly but in a limited manner. Man lives imperfectly but with limitless opportunity for perfection. Insecurity has no place in the life of the enlightened. Only those who are unable to see clearly are afflicted with it. We are not going to experience anything which we are incapable of understanding. The effort to live in the moment and throw away all care pays off. He who deliberately climbs out on a limb and saws it off will surely fly away unharmed! The confidence creates the condition. The security creates the confidence. And faith, hope, and love create the security.

When we see the way clearly, we know who we are and why we are where we are. God will assume the burden of our problems if we just lay them at His feet. He is the only one through Whom we all gain access to our goals. Also, all *personal manifestations* of God (Christ, Buddha, Muhamad, and others) are available for all of us to love, to worship, and to submit our problems to. We hold them in our hearts and thank God for them. Security comes from two elements, faith and love, knowing that our Father loves us and having faith that whatever happens will be for the best good. We have no needs that are not being met.

Now is the only time that we really have. The effort to

keep alive is very important, and we must understand what a privilege this is. If we allow ourselves to give in to appearances, we will be victimized by our emotions and unable to see anything clearly enough. We must be able to weather all storms with faith, hope, and love and eliminate all negative thought. The only thing that counts in any situation is what we think about it. If we are certain in our minds that all *is* well, we will be fulfilling our part of the bargain. Don't think "*was* well" or "*will* be well," but "*is* well." The present is all that counts.

Your problems with lack of faith and insecurity will surely fall away when you learn to live this way. Insecurity is not based on reality but comes from spiritual blindness. To become spiritually enlightened takes a long, long time, but it is the goal we are headed for whether or not we are aware of it. When insecurity is attached to pride, the problems are compounded, but if we can realize the importance of living in the moment, we can overcome any such problem. To be willing to fasten our attention on "now" is to live in faith, accepting all that happens as God's will. This is taking a chance. This is knowing that our beliefs determine the condition of our lives.

But living by such faith often makes us seem crazy in the minds of others.

Yes. This we must assume. However, if we know in our hearts it is right for us, it *is* right for us. Out of this conviction will come the resolution which will alleviate our problems and create spiritual growth of importance. Take a chance! This is what I want to impress upon you. Take a chance on living freely in the moment. Take a chance on faith, hope, and love. The way to live is simple. Relish each moment for itself, knowing that God

wants us to be happy and that the only way to be happy ✗
is to do His will and live in the moment. When we recognize the adventure of life, we are seeing things as they
really are. It is true that the earth is the battleground for
spiritual development, but if we enter the fray to win, we
bring to it the desire-power necessary for success.
Remember, we have heaven on our side, so how can we
lose? Winning means a lot of things, but most of all it
means inner peace, contentment, and happiness. Insecurity is the basis for many faults. If we can throw off
the yoke of insecurity and learn the importance of fulfilling the moment, development follows. We are no longer
involved in negative thoughts of regret and anticipation
which never are concerned with the moment. Living in
the moment is the law here. It is yours by choice. Making
the choice is a growth element. Life is an adventure. The
more we can relish each moment, the more we are growing spiritually. All situations are challenging to one degree or another, but challenging nevertheless.

*Isn't there a difference between what I should be do-
ing and what I am doing in a given moment?*
The only way to be sure we are living properly in the
moment is to live it with an open heart. If we put away
negative thought and relish each moment as precious
because it is unique and will never quite happen the
same way again, we will be allowing all possible benefit
to reach us. Pray for the miracle. Don't be afraid to
express your true feelings. Keep open and receptive.
Know in your heart that all is well. Live as though each
moment is valuable. Keep yourself free from doubt and
fear, and you will be proving yourself worthy of God's
grace. Listen to your heart feelings. They are filled with
faith, hope, and love, and they can show you the way.
Listen to what your heart tells you, and you can't go

wrong. Make certain that you are occupied with either your work with me or your daily tasks, contemplation and prayer, or communication. Incidental time can be utilized in prayer and contemplation. No more insecurity. No more worry and indecision. No more need to protect yourself from coming events, since you now know they will be what God wants for you.

Deterrence

I thought about those who deliberately
choose deterrence, and this prompted my
next question to Richard.

*What happens when we give in to deterrence and live
by our compulsions?*

The purpose of life is lost to those who have succumbed
to self-will. They think that what they want in life—
money, position, acclaim, power—is achieved through
aggression by fair means or foul. The most important
issue in life is getting ahead at all cost. "After all, isn't
this a dog-eat-dog world? Aren't the clever ones faster on
the draw? They are certainly the survivors!" Don't listen
to your compulsions. Try to keep yourself free from deterrence. Construction can always be realized through
imagination and self-control. Nothing is as difficult as it
appears. Our heart feelings are strong enough to carry
us if we will heed them. However, deterrence is a
measure of our development. When we have freed ourselves from compulsion and can live in relative peace
with ourselves, we will know we have grown. This can be
achieved with a check at the source. Whenever we feel
compulsive urgency, we should recognize that it is a
guise to confuse us. We don't really have a need to be
satisfied. We just think we do. If we turn our backs on
these feelings, they will fall away. Holding on to the
feelings is dangerous. It can weaken our resolve.

The energy level of these impulses is high, like a spark

which ignites and burns brightly for a short time. Construction, on the other hand, is more like the air that surrounds the spark, which quietly absorbs its energy and dissipates it. If we remember this, we won't feed the spark with the fuel of our imagination. We will then be able to tolerate the momentary upsurge, knowing that it will soon die out. Let us turn our attention from it and it won't develop. Keeping ourselves open and receptive to spiritual influence will enable us to build a fortress of defense which will diminish deterrence.

Deterrence is a force in the world at large just as construction is a force in the world at large. When we give in to deterrence, we contribute to the overall force of deterrence. Thoughts are things, and when they are coupled with action, they make a considerable contribution to the whole, whether it be to construction or deterrence. All are affected: the giver, the receiver, and the force at large. Our karmic problems are the keys which unlock the Pandora's box of deterrence. Once we have seized upon any one of the keys and opened the box, we are engulfed in the essence of deterrence. The longer we tolerate this atmosphere, the more difficult it becomes to close the lid and lock up the box. The effect is felt by all in our environment. However, deterrence cannot survive for long in the presence of construction. Its effect is diminished by turning our imaginations toward our heart feelings, toward purpose.

We have often heard it said that there is no time like the present, and this is so true. Problems are overcome by facing them now. Procrastination makes life more difficult. The purpose of effort is progress. Don't neglect it. When we feel the least like working, that is when we should be working the hardest. Deterrence has many guises, and one of them is fatigue, the physical inability to do what we should. It is certainly physical, but often old problems bring it about. Keep yourself open and free of worry and fear, optimistic and ready for anything, and you will be able to experience events fully.

We are all children of God, so we must try to foster loving kindness toward all. In this way we combat deterrence. If we allow ourselves to become empty, deterrence can enter the vacuum. If we fill ourselves with constructive harmony and use it to construct our lives from moment to moment, there will be no room for deterrence. Old habits bring back memories of past experiences relating to the habits. If they were constructive, they form a groundwork upon which to build. Memory of past construction is the basis for present constructive action, which, in due time, makes its contribution to the memory book upon which our moral character is built. If, however, our old habits were deterrent, they, too, contribute to our memory book. From every deterrent act a constructive result can come if we learn the lessons being taught.

We cannot discuss vices except in the context in which they are being experienced. If we really believe that nothing that happens to us is as important as what we think about it, we then realize that deterrence becomes such only by our own reaction to an event. Events cannot be deterrent unless we allow them to affect us deterrently. Vices have no reality except through our reactions to the circumstances of our lives. Take sloth, for example. We can be slow and ponderous by nature and not lazy. However, if we realize that we are lazy and that it is holding us back from doing what we really want to do, but we do nothing about it, we are acting deterrently. Acting to satisfy our inner needs could turn our lives around. If, on the other hand, we are slow and ponderous and lacking energy and concentration, but we are also patient, loving, and long-suffering and our hearts are satisfied with our lives, we are not living a slothful, sinful life. We are fulfilling our own plan of life and God's will for us.

Can karmic problems be eliminated by constructive acts alone?

Yes. But the solution is more complicated than you think. To be able to react constructively to all events requires great development. We must cope with emotion and blindness to truth. Such deterrence cannot be eliminated with thought alone. Gradually, with persistence, we can learn to see more clearly. Deterrence doesn't exist in a vacuum. Each person is responsible for his own sins. The subject cannot be discussed in generalizations, only in specifics. There is no formulation. Life isn't like that. People cannot stop everything and change without effort. It takes time and development. To expect it to be otherwise would be like expecting a child to fit into adult clothes.

Christ brought the solution to the karmic problem by showing that love overcomes all. But this does not mean it can be done in one thought or one action. We need to live out this conviction during a lifetime, and then, if our problems are few and our effort is great, we may achieve some result. "Love thy neighbor as thyself." The application of this principle will surely help us. Before Jesus' time, "an eye for an eye and a tooth for a tooth" was accepted moral practice. The command to love our enemies was a whole new and necessary concept, geared toward development. The plan of life is carefully worked out to allow us full rein with our heart feelings. Problems develop when people listen to others instead of themselves. It takes persistent soul searching to sort out our heart feelings from our compulsions. However, we do know ourselves best, and our lives have a purpose which our hearts want to achieve.

Compulsion

Richard had said that freeing ourselves from compulsion was a sign of growth. I asked for further explanation.

What must we learn about compulsion?
Compulsion stems from long-term conditions, which tend to vary from incarnation to incarnation. To understand why compulsion, which is deterrent by nature, exists, we must examine the cause of it in the first instance. The cause is a mirage. It is something that we imagine to be real but that has no reality.

You have said thoughts are things. Why, then, do you say that imaginings are not real? If thoughts are things, isn't imagination real?
Yes, it is true. But its existence as thought doesn't offer us a threat, unless we think it does. I haven't finished with this yet. Compulsions are the residue of serious conditions, which we may be trying to eliminate. They are the smoke which comes with our efforts to put out the fire. Turn away from the smoke, and you won't be affected by its fumes. Remove yourself (change that condition), and you won't have to endure its unpleasantness any longer. We all have some of these feelings. They are part of being human. However, some of us develop stronger resistances and are able to minimize the effects. Others find it more difficult to cope with them. No one need be victimized by them, however. The framework of compulsion is shaky and collapses under

107

pressure. It is essential to recognize this fact. By making a strong initial effort to resist and then turning our attention to other matters, we can minimize its effect.

How can we overcome our compulsions?

First, we must want to overcome them. Second, we supplant them with construction; then they will die and fall away. The construction we must build is filled with all of the heart feelings we possess. When we dig deep for a firm foundation, we find at the bottom of our hearts much that can help us. Knowing ourselves will provide us with the material for a firm foundation, built to last. Compulsion always comes in waves, and the periods in between should be spent shoring up our foundations so that the construction can withstand the storms and continue to be built on. Although we always have the option of starting over, we don't progress very rapidly that way. Work now to firm up your foundation to withstand the battering of the storm of deterrence.

Compulsive acts are not in themselves the problem. They are manifestations of the real problems. One may take to drink through insecurity and lack of faith. One may take to sex through vanity and pride. And even the alcohol and sex are not in themselves wrong. They are only wrongly used, as destructive force, in excess, for the wrong reasons. There is no way to overcome such problems unless we are willing and able to see ourselves honestly. Then an understanding of how to proceed will come to us who ask for it. Living in faith and humility and the security of God's love is what is required. Everyone is born with certain characteristics, some of them inherited and some of them karmic. The inherited ones are intended to help us overcome the karmic ones. We may have strong compulsive desires toward the misuse of sex, alcohol, and drugs, but we may also be given clear, rational minds. The hope could be that our minds will grasp where our compulsions are taking us and we will use our spiritual equipment to overcome them. Compulsion and negative emotion are manifestations of unsolved problems of previous incarnations. They are the deterrent elements which rise to the surface from the deeply buried fundamental problems, our karma. We do not overcome them by attacking them directly. They must be replaced by construction.

Self-knowledge is essential to growth. The solutions to our problems lie within the problems themselves. If we are capable of recognizing our problems, we are also capable of solving them. The solution can be found within the realization. Our spiritual equipment will not fail us. We must put our trust in it. Compulsion need not be taken seriously if we understand its true nature. Its strength derives from a lack of understanding. It comes with great energy, but it cannot prevail for long. It persists only with encouragement. It doesn't give up easily, but if ignored, it disappears. There is a constructive ground to all events, and the compulsive act is no different from any other action. Nothing that happens to us is as important as what we think about it. The way we respond to the rush of compulsion is a clue to our development. Compulsion must feed on us and requires our cooperation to exist. It is a residue of an ongoing problem or even of a problem practically solved. In either case it cannot exist without our help. To the extent that we give in to it, we are keeping it alive. The more we can ignore it, the sooner we are rid of its cause. We need not be victims of compulsion unless we want to be. The choice is always ours. By stepping aside from the situation, we can see it for what it is and what to do about it. The force of the thrust of compulsion lies in its immediacy. If our response is not to respond at all, the feeling will leave us. There is no tensile strength to it. It has only thrust and cannot prevail if ignored.

Once involved, we tend to enjoy our compulsions. Not recognizing who we are contributes to all of our problems. If we accept the fact that we are offspring of God, destined to become perfect through our own efforts, we can also recognize that problems can and will be eliminated if we are true to ourselves and our source. To understand and to accept are basic to our growth and development and essential to achieving our ultimate goal. The pleasure of perversity is illusory. Our true nature must be understood. The reason we are where we are must be grasped, and we must learn how to cope with compulsion and negative thinking. Compulsion cannot win out against construction in the long haul. God has willed it so. Once we are able to act on our understanding, the battle is already half won. Think this over.

What about those who live out their lives compulsively—the drug addicts, the alcoholics, the sexually promiscuous?

This is a very difficult situation to be in. Those who have no feelings of concern or regret for their acts do not know themselves at all. They think their surface reactions to events represent their true nature. How sad it is when we are unwilling to probe our inner beings to find out who we really are. Such compulsion is an effort to overcome the cause (however unconsciously) by attempting to satiate the insatiable. The effort inevitably leads to the state in which we are totally unable to recognize who we are and why we are here. Depending upon where our compulsions have led us, we may be allowed to return to the Place of Preparation to start over again, or we may be sent to the Lower Regions, where much greater effort must be applied in order to get back on firm ground.

Evil

The discussion of deterrence and compulsion made me think of the old-fashioned word "evil."

What exactly is evil?

It is difficult for most of us to separate right from wrong, and there is great uncertainty about which way to go. God's plan is not understood. We are unwilling to believe that we must account for our actions and that nothing goes by unnoticed. Each person's deterrence affects all. Evil is often looked upon as something from without, whereas evil, or rather deterrence, which is its root, comes from within. We tend to classify many events of diverse origin within the same category. Manifestations of evil, such as oppression or catastrophe, do not all stem from the same source, nor are they manifestations of the same circumstances. The problem comes from regarding events from the surface instead of looking within to discover their ingredients. Generalizations are odious. One can only understand events from an individual point of view. Every one of us involved in a calamity is having an experience different from that of everyone else sharing the same event. The reason anyone is present at that moment is individual. In order to examine this subject with any clarity we must realize that thoughts are things. Thoughts, once expressed in either words or action, become reality and, as such, affect events. Since thoughts are matter, they are attracted to like matter. Not only do they alter events by

111

creating changing circumstances, but they are also attracted to the body of related thought, which we shall refer to as good or evil (construction or deterrence). Evil is a fact of life and will remain so for aeons to come. It stems from deterrent thought, and as long as deterrent thoughts exists, evil will exist. It is the result of man's selfish motives.

Free will, the God-privilege given to man, grants us the opportunity to make choices. This privilege carries with it the responsibility to choose right over wrong. Free will and self-will are closely related. Everyone has free will and everyone wants to get ahead, so it is easy to confuse the two and to believe that self-will and free will are synonymous. What difference does it make, really, what we have to do to get ahead? Wouldn't anyone do the same if he could? Aren't the smart ones always on top? These are justifications for all self-willed thought and action. The self-made person is the epitome of success in society today. We all admire aggression. We need it to climb the ladder of success. However, there is no reason why we shouldn't do what we want to do, as long as what we want is what our hearts want too, not what our minds or our compulsions want. If we allow ourselves to be swayed by pressure from without, we will not be able to listen to the inner voice, because it will be crowded out by an overactive mind scheming to get ahead.

The effect of evil is twofold. Those who perpetrate evil are doing themselves real harm. Those upon whom the evil is perpetrated may or may not be affected by it negatively. This depends entirely upon how they react to the event and the circumstances which brought it about. Since there are no accidents, one must learn to accept the fact that all events are purposeful. All who are on earth are there because they have problems to over-come. It is understandable that so many people find the problems more powerful than the qualities they have acquired to overcome them with. They fall back on old habits when put to the test and find themselves reverting and doing just the things they know in their hearts they must not do. Deterrence becomes evil through intensity and development. The problem of pride, for instance, can manifest itself in both simple and complex ways. The degree to which it is allowed to possess a person makes the difference between deterrence and evil. The same is true of all of the problems of mankind. When a combination of such problems manifests in the same individual, he ends up with the ability to project evil upon others, which, of course, redounds upon the individual.

The person who is the victim of evil intent is playing a part in a larger drama than he is aware of. Relationships in this case tend outward into a wider circle than the sphere of an individual's influence. If we become embroiled in an event by what appears to be happenstance, it is because our relationship to the event is essential, however minor or casual it may seem to be. The one opportunity it offers us above all else is to react constructively, accepting the fact that there is something to be learned and gained from the experience. Evil, the manifestation of mankind's thoughts and actions, is a force which is ever-present in the world, just as good is ever-present as a force. Evil and good are the outcome of deterrence and construction. Deterrent thought, which creates evil, and constructive thought, which creates good, are the two polarities of living on earth. We cannot have one without the other. The presence of one implies the presence of the other. Evil is entirely an earthbound condition.

The fulfillment of God's dream depends upon each one of us. Even those who regard themselves as religious often practice archaic concepts of right and wrong and in many ways are no further ahead than the atheists. In fact, he who lives a constructive life—no matter what his beliefs—is doing as much as he can do to fulfill himself. Moral values take on different colors in the light of truth. What is right for one may not be right for another, and what is wrong for one may not be wrong for another. Trying to impose moral restrictions on the masses with the concept that what is right for one is right for all does not allow the individual to grow according to God's plan for him or her. Individuality cannot be denied, no matter what restrictions are put upon it, because its fulfillment is fundamental to our reason for being. But this, too, can be a cause for difficulty, if it is not accompanied by spiritual understanding and the knowledge of our ultimate purpose. The individual who lacks understanding of his potential Godhood is pursuing deterrence through self-will. The urge toward movement either results in growth or else it redounds to our discredit, and entrance into the Lower Regions is the outcome.

The Lower Regions

I had heard of "hellfire," but from the little Richard had said about the Lower Regions, they seemed quite different from what I expected.

Where, exactly, does all this evil and deterrence lead us? What will happen if we don't learn the lessons being taught?

If we are determined to follow deterrence at all costs, at death we earn a special place for ourselves in the Lower Regions. This place is filled with souls who have lost a claim on their purpose. They can no longer realize that they are responsible for their plight. They are filled with deterrent emotions. They could get out of the Lower Regions by changing their state of mind, but the inertia which permeates the place is extremely difficult to combat. The simple desire to change is impossible for most to comprehend. Help is always at hand, but few are able to take advantage of it.

The way we experience the life after life depends upon many elements. An important element is our beliefs. If we believe we deserve hell, or are unworthy of heaven, we may very well experience the place which our beliefs have created. Also, if we have lived a deterrent life, we will probably experience the hell which we have earned. The determining factor is the ratio of good and evil in a life. Many people appear to be bad but have within them elements of love which make a real difference in the outcome. Those of us who suffer from self-doubt and unworthiness or protracted willful compulsions may have serious problems to solve in the next life, starting with an environment embodying the depressive and oppressive elements of our former lives. We did not come well prepared to begin with, and now are only adding to our problems. A person who has been neither constructive nor deterrent and entertains no concept of an afterlife at all may get nothingness, a void, to be filled only by his own generated effort. Help is available, but it takes desire for change to put it into play. The person is blinded to truth by his own thoughts and actions and must experience the environment he himself has created. Those who died clinically and experienced life after life, and were then revived have had a unique opportunity to alter their future by their subsequent thoughts and actions. We can always change the outcome of our lives by a change in attitude. Remember what Christ said to the repentant thief on the cross: "Today shalt thou be with me in Paradise." Even though construction is more powerful than deterrence in the long haul, when great deterrence is concentrated, it has a short-time power which is devastating. We condemn ourselves to the Lower Regions. We are never abandoned there. We abandon ourselves.

Imagine this: You have died and during your lifetime you were only out for yourself. You felt the world owed you all you could get, and you didn't try to understand those around you who could have influenced your thoughts and actions favorably. You were a financial success, and you had had everything you ever wanted. You had cheated on your wife and placated your children with money to get them out of the way. You were admired in society for your aggressiveness and self-sufficiency. You never thought about religion, but you were good to your mother, who had been long widowed. When you died you were an item in the paper and you had a big funeral. No one really mourned you except your mother. All of your family benefited from your death through inheritance and insurance. Where do you suppose you are going now?

I don't really know, because although it seems I have asked for hell, still I have been good to my mother. I guess the Lower Regions.

You think that such a life deserves the pits, and so it would seem. But the glimmer of light which emanates because of love for your mother exists no matter where you find yourself, and this still, small light within you can be observed and nourished by those who are there to help. Your chances are good (though protracted) for recovery into the light of understanding and truth. It is seldom that a life is so completely deterrent that it could not be reconstructed.

Remember this: we create our own hell. We get what we descrve because of our own thoughts and actions. Hell is real. It is not imaginary. It is a well-established condition and environment. People in those regions are not sitting around dreaming of heaven. They think they are where they should be. That is, those who can think at all do. Many have lost all concept of thought or desire or dreams. What they sense is what they know, and the cold, clammy inertia is accepted as normal. The weight of inertia makes it difficult to overcome. Those who come to help, hope for the tiniest spark of energy, love, desire—anything that could be turned into construction. God's servants are always on the lookout for any sign of change.

Imagine that you had lived a relatively stable life. You had raised and educated your children, you had not cheated on your wife. You didn't know how to express your feelings, and you lived a straight-laced life. You had no apparent vices, but you were not a happy man. You felt as though life had passed you by and that you didn't have the opportunity or the will to enjoy your fantasies. Your internal life was chaotic because you wouldn't express your feelings. One day you killed your wife and committed suicide. Where do you suppose you went?

I would have to end up in the Lower Regions, but my basic qualities would enable me to move forward with help.

You are correct. You would recognize the value of energy, however misplaced, and the fact that the shock of murder and suicide can bring us back to understanding more quickly than inertia can. The Lower Regions exist by the grace of God. If there were no such place, there would be no possible solution for many. Those who experience this place, which they deserve, are given the opportunity to understand the working out of moral law and how thoughts and actions are subject to it. He who wants help gets it. If we didn't have the opportunity to suffer the consequences of our actions, we would never learn to see clearly. Anyone who wants change can have it. We are not condemned; we condemn ourselves. We don't have to stay if we want to move on. Hope is ever-present. The love of God permeates this place as it does every other place that exists, and when the blind learn to see at last through their own efforts and the efforts of those who are there to help, they start again to move toward growth and development with the added qualities they have gained from their experience in this place.

The opportunities provided by God's dream of perfection are available to all of us no matter where our efforts have brought us temporarily. No one is given up for lost, no matter how deeply he has mired himself. There is the ever-present possibility that the God within might reach the heart and mind of the poor lost sheep and bring him back into the fold. No one is robbed of the opportunity to achieve ultimate perfection. God wills it so.

Negativism is a form of hell. We who concentrate on error will surely experience hell both here and hereafter. The effects of this state contain the seeds of development. However, if we don't recognize this fact, we will continue down the wrong path until we finally realize what we are doing to ourselves. He who concentrates on error forgets he has a purpose in life and that ultimately he is to reach perfection if he follows God's plan. No one is immune to some negativism, but those who concentrate on it are in for trouble.

The solution to the problems of mankind remains buried in the heart feelings and the fulfillment of heart wishes. Construction can free us from the hell we choose to impose upon ourselves through concentration on error. The way for all is the way of faith, hope, and love. If we believe in the goodness of God, we hope for a successful outcome to all problems, knowing that the problems are purposeful and that the purpose is our own growth. We love our Father and we strive to love all those with whom we come in contact, because we know that everyone influences our own well-being. For all we give in love, we reap a hundredfold. Success in living is achieved through obedience to God. This means living the constructive life in humility, faith, hope, and love. When our will is truly God's will (construction), we are doing all we can to move forward.

Self-will develops all the conditions for hell. Those who choose the selfish, self-willed path will surely arrive in the Lower Regions. Self-will creates a state of hell no matter where we are. The person who doesn't recognize the difference between heart feelings and compulsion will always go with compulsion, which is more on the surface and well established from use. Probing our hearts to learn about ourselves and our real needs is a difficult task at best, and extremely difficult for one who looks only to self-gratification as the solution to his problems. The Lower Regions are full of well-meaning people who got off on the wrong foot. If we mistake selfish motive for personal gain and we start down the path of "me first," we are going to end up in a mire.

There is a world of difference between self-development and selfish motive. If you respond to peer pressure with acquiescence, you are losing sight of your own uniqueness in an effort to become one of the gang. What is right for others may very well be wrong for you. The whole question of the functioning of moral law is brought into play through our decisions for or against what our heart feelings tell us. The insecure person is sure to seek advice from his more aggressive friends, equating that quality with truth instead of looking within to find his own desires to follow. Such people often seek psychiatric help and end up blaming their parents for their problems instead of recognizing that they chose their parents and that their present circumstances are meaningful. Those who try the wrong solutions for the wrong reasons end their lives unable to see clearly in spite of all their effort. They look upon what happens to them as bad luck or someone else's fault, and ignore the construction which lies beneath events. They usually rely on intellectual jargon and formula solutions, which pass for an intelligent approach to life. They may mean well, but they have put their heads ahead of their hearts, and they are the losers. Even though we find ourselves in difficult circumstances when we make the transition from the Place of Preparation to earthly life, our energy will aid us and bring us to understanding in time. You have heard it said that the road to hell is paved with good intentions. So it is!

I wonder how, with the preparation which has been made, one can end up so badly. Why is it that those who have a good intellect and come prepared to grow go so wrong?

The one most important element in growth is to know ourselves. Those who have never been willing to find what lies beneath, for fear they won't like what they see, are unable to proceed with spiritual growth. They seek approval by aping those around them who have stronger motivations and thereby lose sight of themselves. Intellectual prowess is not the solution to spiritual problems. Love, sense of truth, and intuition are everyone's tools. Many fail to use them. Free will dictates that everyone must make his own decision concerning his reincarnating readiness. Many often do so ill-prepared.

Moral Law

Where we end up after death obviously depends, according to Richard's teaching, upon the function of moral law, about which I had a vague understanding. I asked Richard for more information.

What particulars should I know about moral law?
Although what is right for you may be wrong for another, this does not preclude the function of moral law, which affects everyone. You have heard about cause and effect, action and reaction, compensation and retribution, but what I want to talk about now is something quite different. I want to talk about usury. Yes, I said usury. Now you have looked it up: the dictionary defines it as interest, a premium paid for a loan. Do you see that it has possible moral implications? I want you to understand how this is so.

When anyone decides to reincarnate (and it *is* that person's decision), he does so with the knowledge that the outcome of this act will mean either progress or regression for him. The privilege of being able to move forward in this way carries with it the responsibility to do so. Along with the "loan" of an incarnation goes the necessity to pay "interest" for the privilege. Usury must be understood in the living out of an incarnation. All actions bring with them their own specific reactions. For every cause there is an effect. We are compensated in kind for a constructive act, and deterrence brings with it retribution.

Usury is interest paid for a loan. If we are given something we need (an incarnation), we must be willing to pay for it. What we must pay as compensation for this loan is obedience to the will of God (construction). If we follow the constructive way during an incarnation, we are paying as we go, and the achievements of the incarnation are ours fully and forever. If, on the other hand, we don't pay the interest at all or even partially, we end up with a debt on the interest and the loan unrealized as well. We find ourselves in a far worse state than we were in before we decided to take this step. The function of moral law is infallible. Woe unto him who reincarnates unprepared! All of the moral laws break down to one: usury. We must pay for the privilege of growth with obedience.

The facts are these: we are given the circumstances of an incarnation, which, if lived out constructively, will secure for us a specific gain. We will be the richer and more secure for the experience. We must pay for the privilege of a loan one way or another. If we pay as we go by following our hearts and doing what we set out to do, we will have paid back both the loan and the interest in the end. If we do not pay as we go, we will still owe the loan plus the interest which has accrued over the span of the incarnation, so the total owed is far greater than the original loan. Moral law dictates this. We are responsible for all our thoughts and actions and for all the reactions which they cause. There is compensation for all constructive thought and action, and retribution for all deterrent thought and action. By fulfilling our part of the plan, we pay back, with interest, the original loan of the experience. Failing to do so, we then owe not only the original loan, but the interest too, which has increased with every deterrent thought and action.

The way to live free of debt is to live constructively. By

constructing with the thoughts and actions which stem from our heart feelings, we utilize the loan and add qualities which become permanent members of the structure we are striving to erect (a unique, perfect being). If we are able to live our lives true to our inner feelings and desires, we will inevitably emerge from an incarnation with all debts paid. However, we are not expected to be perfect. We are expected to believe in ourselves and our intrinsic worth, and we are expected to live in love and harmony with others. We are expected to try and try and try!

Our imperfections will not deter us if our intentions are right. Try not to let yourself become fearful or negative in any way. This is the open door to deterrence. Humility stems from an understanding of who we are and what is being done for us to help us reach our goals. Our unpaid debts and interest become our karma. The interest compounds the debt. The problems we have wanted to overcome become far greater problems as a result of our own thoughts and actions. Moral law comes into play at every decision and action of our lives. An example of the working of moral law is cause and effect. Like action and reaction, it has to do with us and the outcome of our reactions to events. The way we react to an event is in itself the creation of circumstances which will develop into an event. Moral law is unswerving, constant.

You have spoken to me about cause and effect, action and reaction, parallels, retribution, and supply and demand. Tell me more about these in relation to moral law.

You have come up with five topics, and I shall attempt to clarify them for you. All of these are natural laws, but they are not all moral laws. We must separate in our minds the intention of the law. Cause and effect have to do with circumstances and events. The circumstances are the cause and the event is the effect. Circumstances alter events. Action and reaction are similar but different. The event is the action, and your response is the reaction. The effect of cause and effect becomes the action of action and reaction. The reaction of action and reaction creates circumstances which become the cause of cause and effect. Circumstances create events (cause and effect), and events create circumstances (action and reaction). The only time these natural laws become moral laws is when they are applied to human behavior.

Human beings are the only creatures on earth who can make moral choices which affect their spiritual growth. The knowledge can prove helpful if we recognize our role in the scheme of things. By contributing construction to the circumstances of our lives, we are participating positively in the functioning of the laws of nature and utilizing this function to our own benefit. If, on the other hand, we contribute deterrence to the circumstances of our lives, we are participating in the functioning of the laws of nature in a negative way, and we are receiving the result of their function to our detriment. The laws function according to their nature, and we receive what we deserve in all situations. The laws are fair and unbiased and based upon God's will (construction). If we contribute construction, we are living according to God's will and are benefiting from the function of the laws. The purpose of all natural laws is to set things back into construction. They are the machinery through which God's will functions. Those who do not live constructive lives are not punished for their acts. They punish themselves. The working out of the law brings them into their problems. However, God provides a way out. To recognize our problems is to see the possibility of a solution (which always exists). We are never completely lost. We have just taken a devious path.

Under what circumstances should I take an action?
The only way to act is to react. Never take overt action when the circumstances don't suit you. The idea is to try to learn why the circumstances are as they are. When we have found the construction which lies buried, we should wait until an event or events occur to which we are required to react. We will then make decisions which, if constructive, will affect our development favorably.

Decisions

Thinking about all of the trouble we can get ourselves into and where it can lead us, I realized that our decisions—our contribution to personal growth—must affect the outcome of our lives profoundly.

What do I need to know about decisions?

Our decisions are the most important acts in our lives. Everyone has both a privilege and a responsibility in this regard. The responsibility is to ourselves and our development, and the privilege is the means through which the development is achieved. Don't become alarmed at any event in your life, no matter how it may appear. What you think about it is the most important element. At the base of all events lies construction, and our job is to find it. Keep free of negativism. It affects reactions to events and subsequent decisions. Negativism and construction are diametrically opposed and cannot coexist. Negativism cannot compete with construction, but it can take over when construction isn't present. Since we are responsible for making our own decisions, we do contribute to the circumstances of our lives and to the events which are their culmination. Try always to let yourself go, to become free inside and make decisions which are in the interest of construction only. This won't be difficult if you just remember that all events are purposeful and have a constructive base.

If we assume responsibility for our own decisions,

does this mean that we can go our own self-sufficient way? No! It means that our responsibility is for our own welfare. Learning to make constructive decisions is essential to growth. The choice between right and wrong, knowing what is right for us as well as what is wrong for us, brings about our development and the realization of our goals. Decisions are the cornerstones of character, and if we follow the constructive path, our development will come about as planned. To live out our lives as planned is a mark of development. God's dream is realized through such effort. If we choose to be servants and messengers of God, our decisions will reflect this choice and serve to move us ever forward toward our ultimate goals.

Try always to withhold decisions which are judgmental of others. Opinions and decisions are not related. Judgment of others has nothing to do with constructive thinking. Since we can never really know anyone else fully, it follows that any judgment we make concerning others cannot reflect the whole truth and is therefore not constructive. Our decisions affect our attitude toward life. Those who decide in favor of self-serving actions are not going to perceive accurately. If we keep our goals in mind and if we understand who we are and why we are where we are, our decisions are simple. The only way we can be certain our decisions are right is by listening to our heart feelings. If we decide in favor of these deepest feelings, and if we are certain our decisions are constructive, then we must know that all is well.

The first time you decided in favor of your heart feelings was the beginning of the development of your character. When your heart decided to follow my advice and ignore your illness, you brought on the circumstances which put you where you are now. [See Postscript.] Above all, you needed to learn obedience in order to experience humility. Through your obedience to my wishes your future development was assured, no matter how things appeared. Your present condition is a growth factor. When you think of what this has gained you in understanding and clarity of vision, you can realize that following our hearts, no matter how foolish it may appear on the surface, is the only way to enlightenment. Each of us has a job to do and making the right decisions affects the outcome.

Obedience

I wondered how decision making relates to
obedience to God's will.

What exactly does obedience to the will of God mean?
The way to perfection is through obedience to the will of
God. This is accomplished by aligning our wills with the
will of God (construction). It is essential to recognize the
kinship between ourselves and God. If we establish construction as the bulwark of our own thoughts and actions, then we are automatically fusing our wills with
God's will. Obedience is working to see clearly and acting upon what we see. Whenever you think of the times
when deterrence has had the upper hand, when self-will
has victimized you and gloom and doom have pre-
dominated, you also realize that although this condition
has happened with great frequency, it has always dis-
sipated and left you with periods of comparative calm.
This happens because even though deterrence is power
ful in its attack on the weakened will, its force soon
dissipates as the strength of God's love again asserts
itself. We can eliminate this vacillation by learning to
react constructively to the events of our lives. We will
find that it is the reactions to events which set the
wheels of deterrence into motion. There is always a
choice to be made in the exercise of free will.

Why not expedite your development instead of allowing deterrence to take its toll? We must be open and
receptive and listen to the inner voice. It is our own

133

source of truth, our own God relationship, our individual help. Our inner voice may be lodged in the heart, but we must keep an open heart to hear it. Our own individual source of security, contentment, love, and power lies in the heart and is expressed through the inner voice. You now recognize that your primary obligation is to our work together, this learning about yourself. To be able to do the work you must have the energy, the will, and the time. It is, then, our health, our desires and beliefs, and our work habits which must adhere to the will of God, the rules for growth, construction. We must examine what we do and feel and think in relation to this, and check whether we need any changes in order to adhere to the rules. There is great freedom in obedience, because in obeying the will of God, we are no longer slaves to self-will and compulsion. The way is cleared for growth.

Obedience to God's will involves many things. First of all, we know that since the nature of God's will is construction, everyone who lives a constructive life is obedient to God's will. Second, we know if we follow our heart feelings, we will be doing what our spirit (the God within) wants of us, and we know that this will be constructive. Obedience to our inner being fulfills our purpose this time. Also, if we are obedient to the needs of our bodies, we will be able to do what we have come to do more efficiently. Our eventual goal is perfection, but in order to reach this state, we must achieve humility and accept our true relationship to our Maker. Obedience is understanding right from wrong and following right. Obedience to our heart feelings can lead us to the right occupation and offers us the opportunity to live a productive life. Our heart feelings are the wishes of our eternal being. We have come to develop certain qualities which we need. Following our heart feelings gives us the opportunity to live out those qualities and give them quantity in the process. This makes them a permanent part of our being.

Life is based on some unchanging and unchangeable facts. These facts exist whether or not we understand or believe them. We are immortal. We will live forever. Once life is created, it never dies. It changes form as conditions change, but there is a constant and continuing thrust toward growth and development, which continues until the ultimate is reached. Evolution exists. Everything is evolving. All matter has life and is in a constant state of change. Nothing is destroyed. It merely changes form. Immortality is closely linked to free will. Since we are going to live forever, and since we do have the ability to make choices (every decision is an expression of free will), our future depends upon obedience to God's will (construction). By being obedient to our inner feelings, we are following the formula for growth and development. Obeying our health needs makes our bodies more useful to us as long as we have need for them.

Obedience, then, has to do with many facets of being a person. Be careful, however, that you don't become obedient to your compulsions and your faults. Self-knowledge is the key to understanding this fact. What we really want gives us the clue to what we should do in life. Our way leads to our goal. Our goal becomes clearer as we live our lives from day to day, being true to our hearts. Follow your heart and you will be living a constructive life, obedient to the needs of your eternal spirit. We must allow our inner feelings to surface in order to understand what we really want out of life. We can't follow our hearts if we are not sure what our hearts really want. Know yourself and you will know what to do with your life.

Illness

I wondered whether the statement "We need what we get and get what we need" was true even of illness.

Does illness come from wrongdoing or from need?
Our health is a barometer of internal weather conditions. Our emotional lives and our physical lives are inseparable. Our spiritual lives and our physical lives are not necessarily inseparable. Illness is not necessarily an indication of karmic problems. Illness can serve many purposes, and only the person who is experiencing the illness can possibly know which purpose applies to his case. He may not realize it until after the illness has run its course, or even after he has experienced repeated illnesses. Since serious illness is often the means of transition out of your world, it is usually regarded in that light whenever it occurs. Through the experience of illness much can be learned about ourselves and the good which is contained within it. Whether it is self-imposed or imposed from without, it happens because there is a need for change, and through the illness one is given the opportunity to change for the better. The span of a life is set, and if we accomplish what is expected of us during that span, we are living according to plan. However, there are many reasons why things don't work out as planned. Illness can serve as either a corrective measure or a terminating measure, depending upon which is the most con-

137

structive. It takes on a different light when we recognize that every event is purposeful. There are no accidents. We get what we need, and we need what we get. By searching for solutions to problems, we find the solutions within the problems. Illness, then, embodies construction, and our job is to find it in order to receive the benefit it offers.

How illness serves to bring us to an understanding of ourselves and our true needs is a fascinating subject. It is a blessing in disguise. Those who go through it are capable of benefiting from it. Everything depends upon us, our attitude, our response, our thinking process, our understanding, and our faith. The benefits are present within the problem, but it is up to us to discover and act upon them. Those who overcome serious illnesses and benefit from them are utilizing the growth factors involved in illness. Their achievements move them forward with special emphasis. Those who have serious illnesses which they don't understand and from which they learn nothing about themselves may be afflicted over and over again as a means of bringing them to constructive thinking. All effort is made to teach us to see ourselves clearly and to act upon our understanding. The reaction of the individual determines which experience he is having. Illness is beneficial, no matter how it appears. The seeds for growth are present, and even terminal illness serves as preparation for what is to come. The way we react to illness reflects the way we are bound to react to the disorientation which takes place at death. Those who accept in faith reap the rewards in all events.

We need to become more and more sure of ourselves in order to understand the benefits which come our way in whatever guise they appear. Being sure of ourselves means knowing who we are, why we are where we are, and what we have to do. When this is so, nothing can shake our confidence and our faith in the goodness of God. There is a purpose for every event. Whatever we are given to experience is intended for our growth and development. No real harm can come to one who believes beyond the shadow of a doubt that all is well. By living in faith, hope, and love, one rids oneself of fear. When we are hit with illness which we don't understand, we must try to live each day for itself in faith. Otherwise we will be buffeted about with every wind and storm. Each morning when we awaken, if we know we are all right, this is all that counts. Time will give us the answers to our problems if we are open and receptive to suggestion. Situations of fear, uncertainty, and incompleteness must be lived out in faith. Since all the hairs on our heads are numbered, what have we to fear except fear itself? Living in faith enables us to grow according to plan.

Is it possible that events are just activity with no purpose and no consequences? Certainly not. He who gains nothing from his experiences doesn't believe they have value. Accepting the fact that all events are purposeful, it follows that our only concern is to learn the purpose and the construction which lie within. Everything happens in the present. How we adjust to the present is how we live our lives, and what we gain from life depends upon how we live in the present. Illness is an important element in spiritual growth. Through the experience we can learn much about God's love, which we might never be aware of otherwise. The whole purpose of such an experience is understanding. If we can see that everything is really all right in spite of the way it appears, we are understanding truly. We do need what we get, and we do get what we need. This truth must be understood if we are to move forward. There is no point in trying to predict the future. We know that the future comes from the present.

Faith

From all Richard had told me, it seemed that faith was the prerequisite of constructive living. I thought I needed to understand this point better.

Just how important is faith to our lives here on earth? What good are talents without peace of mind? No good at all. I have tried for some time to make you aware of this fact. What must be learned is not as important as what has been learned and forgotten. You have known peace of mind, and you can know it again with just one factor. This factor is faith. If you remember, in the days when you were secure under stress, you were depending upon your faith in the goodness of God. This is the most important thing one can learn. If we do believe in the goodness of God, we can accept everything that happens in the light in which it is given, knowing that insecurity comes from a lack of clear vision.

People are capable of doing anything they really want to do. We can bring about any condition we desire. Our own belief is what makes it happen. If we believe in the goodness of God, we believe that He wants only good for us. If we believe we can reach our ultimate goal, we will. This means we can realize any goal whatever along the way if we believe and trust enough and keep the faith in constructive thought and prayer (an expression of humility). There is nothing which is impossible with this plan of life. Obstacles are present only because we allow them to be present. Everything works out for good ultimately, but we can help to bring it about now if we think and act constructively. This is the most important lesson we can possibly learn.

Faith is an element we cannot live without. In fact, it is so much a part of our everyday lives that we tend to forget about it. We know without giving it a thought when we go to bed at night that it will be morning when we wake up. We are certain that spring will follow winter, that the sun and moon will rise and set, and that there is an ebb and flow in all of life. Indeed, our own well-being is dependent upon faith that our hearts will continue to function. The miracle of the human body is taken completely for granted. We have faith in our very existence.

Since we are willing to have faith in the physical functioning of life, why not have faith in the spiritual functioning of life as well? Since we are here, why not trust that everything will turn out all right here? We know we've learned from our mistakes, so even they are not so bad. It is always possible to cope with difficulties when they are upon us. What does it mean to be here for spiritual growth? It means we are here to develop in the process of living.

If it is true that we learn from our mistakes and the events in our lives, what is it that brings this about? Consider this: The learning process is based on faith— faith in our ability to see the value in the lessons taught from our mistakes and faith in the fact that the base of every event is constructive. If we are being taught to see more clearly through our errors, then there must be love at the core of life, love which wants so earnestly for us to learn that lessons will be taught us through events until we come to recognize the constructive thrust of life. This is the love of God. Events are culminations of specific circumstances. How we react to them is crucial to our development. Our hearts are full of love, ready to be put to use if we open up and allow them to express themselves. If we want to achieve our goal, we must try, open up, trust, be vulnerable, have faith.

Trust is the basis of faith, and faith is essential to living according to God's will. Trust is related to our ability to comprehend the nature of things. If we truly believe that all events have a constructive base, that things are not what they seem, and that everything is really all right, we are indeed living in the essential trust in the goodness of God and in His love for us. Trust, then, is the groundwork upon which we build our beliefs. Without faith, we are subject to every negative emotional whim and victims of all karmic problems.

Faith and hope are both elements of the present. They go hand in hand. Faith emanates from our belief in the goodness of God. Hope emanates from our desire that all will develop according to plan. Faith places its emphasis on God and His attitude toward us. Hope places its emphasis on mankind and its attitude toward God. Both faith and hope are essential elements to the developing soul. One without the other is incomplete.

Prayer

**Richard had often remarked that prayer is
necessary to the development of earth life.**

*Is prayer a necessary part of your life in the Place of
Preparation?*

Prayer here is a state of being. We are what we feel, so
there is no need to ask for help. The help we need is
generated in our own thought and materialized that
way. Help is available for the imagining alone here.
Where you are it is available for the imagining plus the
asking. The only time we petition God is when we pray
for you on earth.

*What is the most effective and beneficial form of
prayer?*

Prayer is a very potent tool and can be utilized to great
benefit by you there and by us here alike. I have said we
get what we need (the circumstances of our lives) and
what we want (our heart feelings lead us to our purpose).
If our prayer life is built around our true needs and our
true wants (not what our compulsions dictate) and if the
basis of our prayer life is "Thy will be done," we will find
our prayers answered in a productive way. Fervor is very
important if we are to achieve the best results. A vivid
imagination, channeled in the direction of our true
wants and our true needs and delivered with fervent
intensity, will achieve a constructive result. However, if

145

we use the same tactics for selfish motives toward deterrent ends, we will also be getting what we want and what we need. But since what we want and what we need in this situation are not the same, the results on the surface are deterrent. Nevertheless, whether or not a lesson has been learned from deterrence, the end result has the possibility of being constructive. Since we always get what we need, and since what we need in this case is to learn a lesson about prayer used for selfish motives, if we learn that lesson we are put back on the constructive path. We reap what we sow, but the bottom line of all events is construction. God so wills it.

Devote time to prayer every day. Pray for all that is close to your heart. Pray for those near and dear to you. Pray for guidance and pray for health. We pray for you, and we want you to pray for us. There is real value in praying for those close to our hearts. Don't be mechanical. Be fervent, and it will benefit all for whom you pray.

Prayer is an expression of humility. It is not something that can be turned on and off to effect. We gain from prayer through persistence. It takes the application of energy to desire to pay off, but we must be careful what we are praying for. I repeat: prayer directed toward a productive purpose is beneficial. However, prayer directed by selfish motives can also be realized, but to the detriment of the individual. This experience can teach humility. Pride has nothing to do with construction.

Our prayers, if powerful and persistent, will be answered, but woe to him who wants foolish things! There is a profound lesson to be learned here. We can influence the events of our lives with the application of sufficient energy in the direction of our desires, but it behooves us to want construction, or else we will interfere with the plan of our lives and bring about deterrence. Circumstances alter events, and persistent prayer, directed with energy, is influential.

It seems to me it might be difficult to know whether our prayers are truly constructive.

By listening to what our hearts really want, we will know. Pray for your desires which lie at the bottom of your heart and you will never go wrong.

What do you mean by "persistent prayer"? Do you mean praying for a long time?

No, I mean it should be a constant, persistent, and powerful petition. Time is not the factor. If healing is what we want, we must fill our bodies with the power of God and call upon that power to heal us. That is enough. The power understands the necessary differentiation. This form of prayer is important to your growth now. Do it daily. Success at prayer requires faith and trust in the goodness of God. The motivating force is the knowledge that help is at hand. Prayer in any form should be a fervent petition for help toward realizing our desires and needs. We must release energy into our desires for benefit. The intensity with which we engage ourselves in this endeavor is the key to the result. Much can be achieved through prayer. If, in the process of trying to satisfy our inner needs and desires, we are met with difficulties which we cannot solve, the solutions can be found in prayer. We need what we get and we get what we need. Energy is the essential ingredient. Desire is the motivator. We must make sure that our requests are related to our inner feelings and not some frivolous surface concern and certainly not our compulsions. Petitions for the wrong reason may be answered, but they can only cause us trouble, unless we can learn the lesson which is being taught.

*I don't understand the idea of getting what we need
and having to pray for it too.*

We get what we need at any given moment. The need
relates to understanding the situation we are in and
what we can do about it. If we are willing to live our lives
without learning about ourselves, our desires, our
faults, our deepest wishes and needs, we are living an
unfulfilled life and losing sight of our reason for being.
What we need, then, is circumstances which will bring
us up short, shock us into reevaluating our condition,
and force us to recognize the folly of our ways. This is
what we need, so the circumstances of our lives bring
about events which will serve this purpose. There are no
accidents. All events are purposeful, and the basis of all
events is construction. It is through God's plan of life
that we are able to cope with the problems we have given
ourselves and progress toward our goals.

Why should we have to pray?

The only way to participate fully in God's plan is to
recognize who we are and why we are where we are. As
we come to understand that everything stems from the
love of God, we feel humility in the truest sense of the
word. We know that we are merely incomplete fragments
of God, but that His love and His will make it possible for
us ultimately to become perfect parts of a perfect whole.
We realize that we need all the help we can get, and
learning to ask for it is part of our development.

God the Father wants us to express our cooperation
and intention, and one way to clarify this is through
prayer. To ask for help, knowing how much we need it, is
to put our relationship to our Father in proper perspective. We influence the circumstances and events of our
lives by our attitude toward them. If we are living a

constructive life, then what we want becomes what we need. Prayer helps to bring this about.

All prayer must contain the petition "Thy will be done." Praying for foolish and selfish things only leads to trouble; what we are asking for and what we need become entirely different because our foolish desires cause us to need to see the error of our ways. Remember, we get what we need, so subsequent events will reflect this need in one way or another. The lesson will continue to be taught until we learn to see more clearly and change our attitude toward our ways. The opportunity for change is always present. Everyone can communicate with God through prayer. In using this means of communication, we often find our questions answered on the spot but don't understand how. This is brain impingement, and it comes about through the opening-up process which prayer induces. Prayer, then, can mean talking and listening, a process often referred to as meditation. Such communication brings us close to the spiritual sources which generate the eternal values of all of life. It is food for the soul and provides us with the nourishment necessary for the exercise of living each day constructively.

Does it matter how I pray? Is there a proper structure for prayer?

Yes. Always start out with the expressions of gratitude for each day and what it brings in understanding. Try to let yourself go freely with the feeling of being at-one with all of life. Concentrate on the moment and direct the energy which develops toward God's plan of perfection for all. Examine your heart feelings in order to expose all problems to the light of love, so you will be able to cope with them with greater understanding. Bring out your feelings and let them assume their rightful relationship to your life, but don't allow emotionalism to creep in since it is your needs and desires which are important now. Once your heart feelings are fully explored, you can raise your petition, using as much concentrated energy as possible. This will come about automatically if you are working fully.

Should worshiping God be an integral part of our lives?

Most certainly. The reason we exist is God's plan. There would be no us, nor any opportunity for us to develop to perfection, but for God's love and His desire to create life, individual life in abundance, to live in the glory of eventual Godhood. Love Him in your heart and express that love outwardly toward those with whom you come in contact—His children, your kin. Try to reflect the love which is lavished on you in your contact with others. Be grateful for the privilege of becoming (which God has bestowed on us all).

You may think it is difficult to direct such feelings toward a Being Who is really all beings, Who is not personified. But what you are not considering is that God is as personal as all of the personalities He has created put together. Think of yourself as a tiny atom of a cosmic Being, God, God the Father (the omnipotent, omniscient Creator of the universe), God the Son (the perfect ones, Christ and those others who have founded the great religions), and God the Holy Ghost (the voice within, the God in us, our hearts' being). By relating ourselves to any and all of these in personal ways, we are worshiping through our understanding and gratitude. This relationship should be on an intimate level. God wants us to express what's in our hearts so we can be helped toward our goals. The teaching of Christ shows us how to live our lives. He can help us through prayer. The Holy Spirit lies within us and can be understood by self-examination, an essential ingredient of our prayer lives.

The act of prayer and meditation (self-examination) should be daily practice. Never fail to petition God or the holy ones or your heart for the help you feel you need. The clearer your understanding of your true needs, the more you can be helped to progress. The true act of worship is a state of being. The worshipful person is one who keeps his mind where his heart is. By becoming at-one with our heart feelings, our priorities are clarified and our wills relate to God's will. Harmony is the true expression of God's love, and if we seek to live in harmony with others, we are living according to plan. The manifestations of harmony—peace of mind, serenity, faith, humility, hope, and charity—become the groundwork upon which we build our lives. The place of worship is the center of our being. The outward trappings are valuable only as reflections of an inner state.

The practice of religion is a personal and private matter. No one is in a position to tell another how to worship. It is an expression of love, devotion, and humility directed toward the Source, God the Father, by His children, each in his or her own way. The diversity of expression pleases God because it is a manifestation of individuality and at-one-ment (atonement) at the same time.

Grace

I was learning that the opportunity for change is always present.

How is opportunity brought about?

Grace brings the whole function of reincarnation to light. It is the ever-present opportunity to change, to move forward, to learn to see clearly and act upon our understanding. No matter how mired down we might become in self-centered deterrence, we can always change for the better. Life is by its very nature developing, growing, evolving, and becoming. No matter how we live our lives, we live in a state of grace because the opportunity for change—for betterment, for growth—is always present. All action can be turned to good, and growth is present in all experience. This is made possible by the grace of God, the ever-present condition of construction available to all.

Life continues forever once it is created, and perfection is its goal. To achieve the goal, we need the opportunity to get back on track after having strayed. This opportunity is provided by grace, that element of construction which turns everything to good. Can you imagine a life lived forever in deterrence? God cannot and did not in His concept of Life. He provides a safe ground for all by enabling everything to be turned to construction. This may be beyond your present comprehension, but it is a fact.

The way to help ourselves is to help others. God knows

and decrees it through grace. The opportunity exists for us to become better and more lucid in our daily tasks. It is up to us to discover it. The entire reincarnational cycle is built on the premise that help is always at hand. Our future depends upon our present. Our present must be lived constructively. This means working with the circumstance of any given moment to fulfill it to the best of our ability. God offers us the opportunity to make something valuable out of the moment through our concentrated attention on it, or to waste it by putting our minds elsewhere, not really living out the moment. It is up to us to understand that we are offered opportunity at all times.

The knowledge that we have help at hand is essential to growth, but help cannot get through to us completely if we are not fully present in the moment. If we are fully involved in "now," help can reach us "now." All events are meaningful and offer help in the form of opportunity, to react in either a constructive or deterrent manner. God's grace also provides this opportunity. The nature of grace is the nature of the function of reincarnation. It is difficult to grasp the fact that opportunity is offered in all circumstances when we observe the seeming difficulties of so many lives. But the only life we can really see clearly (if we are seeing clearly) is our own. No one else is equipped to make clear judgments about the circumstances of our lives but ourselves. No one else can see the real value in the difficulties we have because only we can know what our needs are and what our hearts really want. It is essential to understand this fact so that we can learn to deal with the opportunities with which we are being presented from day to day.

Let yourself go and stop giving in to outside pressures, and you will find God's grace. Let go of all crutches, all braces and supports of any kind, and just call upon yourself to *be*. You will learn what grace is all about. Accept all events as construction and live the circumstances of your life in obedience, without trying to assert your ego, and you will learn what freedom really is. Grace is the privilege of all. If it were not so, we would be left to our own devices and would end up living in the eternal hell we would have created for ourselves. Remorse would do us no good and repentance would not be possible. But for God's grace we would all end up in a state of perdition. We can keep ourselves free from harm by realizing our relationship to our Father and living in faith. Grace makes it possible for everything to work out according to plan. It is up to us to keep our selfish concerns out of it. Living in faith allows grace to be fully realized. We must learn how to live each day.

Built into the structure of daily life is the ever-present possibility for change. There is no limit to this opportunity. You might wonder what opportunity the controlled, monotonous life in prison offers a man. He has time to think. How he utilizes that time is crucial to his development. There are opportunities to learn skills, but the most important opportunity concerns his attitude toward himself and his environment. He must examine himself and recognize why his life has gone wrong and want to correct his faults. Even though his chances may seem slim, his life is unique, and the reasons for being where he is are both individual and meaningful. If he can get past the compulsion and deterrence to his true heart feelings, he will be able to see that his reactions to the circumstances of his life brought him where he is.

If we really want something different and better we can have it, but only if we change our reactions. Opportunity is ever-present. God's grace abounds. Avail yourself of it and you can be the person you set out to be.

Opportunity is present in each moment. The avenues are many. Growth is the purpose of life, and God never fails us.

It is important to start where we are. Don't try to shift your environment in your efforts to advance. Rather, look for the construction which lies at the base of your present circumstances and react to that. From this foundation all else will develop as it should. The conditions of our lives will change as our attitudes change. Work with your spiritual equipment, and you will be able to build a life worthy of your Father's love.

Our efforts are not solitary. Everyone has help through others. Our efforts and the efforts of others coincide at specific junctures and then proceed. This meshing of energy supplies the participants with added factors which help in the accomplishment of the tasks at hand. This opportunity is the element of grace we share in all our relationships, however casual. The simple sharing of mutual concern, respect, and love is a value of importance, a beautiful experience, an element of God's grace.

We learn more about the goodness of God by trusting and believing in the beneficial outcome of all events. Those who know the peace of God recognize it as a blessing bestowed upon the faithful. Grace prevails and we all are privy to it. However, the problems which surround us often blot out the horizon and prevent us from seeing clearly. The opportunity to benefit from what we learn is always present in grace. Giving and receiving are also elements of grace. Growth is the purpose of life, and both giving and receiving are elements of the growth factor. We become more cognizant of our potential by living fully in the moment. In this way we learn what our priorities are. If we seek perfection (and this is everyone's eventual goal), we will not find it by reaching out and searching elsewhere. We will find the way by staying close to home and searching within for the elements with which to fill each moment. Peace comes *Peace* from accepting our present circumstances as the most | important elements of our growth. By examining them | we realize that constructive action doesn't mean running away from the circumstances because we don't like them or they make us uncomfortable or they are not what we think we deserve. It means looking at them, maybe for the first time, for what they really are, the elements of our development. This realization will enable us to react constructively. We need these elements or we wouldn't have them. See what they offer you. Respond to them constructively and you will surely grow.

How does this opportunity to change merge with the plan of our lives?

Our life plan is one of intent. The events of our lives are the culminations of the circumstances of our lives, which result from our choice of parents, and are conditioned by our own thoughts and actions. Our heart feelings coincide with the plan of our lives. We are here to satisfy our real needs as expressed through our heart feelings, and the plan of our lives is designed to achieve that purpose. Even though the opportunity to change is always present, we should make sure that our desire to change is based on an understanding of ourselves and our real needs. Understanding ourselves is basic to all real growth. If our lives are to change through our decisions, it should be for the better, the constructive (God's will) way.

Love is the active factor behind the grace of God. All opportunity is motivated by love. Without love there would be no life. Those who practice charity toward

others are those who recognize the charity which has
been lavished on them. To give and to receive is the same
act of love, involving living beings in a reciprocal way.
Those who love and respect others love and respect
themselves. If we recognize the God in ourselves, we can
also see the God in others and realize that we are all one
in God and in love. God's grace is activated by love, and if
it is received in love, the giving and the receiving become
one and the same act of love. God's grace is om-
nipresent, and when we concentrate our attention on
the moment, we are utilizing it fully and shedding all
regret and worry, using God's grace constructively. If we
spend "now" working for constructive harmony, doing
what our hearts want, we are acting within the
framework of the love and will of God and we are doing all
we possibly can toward our development. Indeed, no
other action can be more beneficial than this. "Now" is
the only moment of reality.

Now

This business about realizing the moment intrigued me.

What more must I learn about "now"?

Now is the time for action. If we act on our heart interests now, we will always be doing God's will. The best way for each of us is his or her own way. Each of us is unique. Therefore, the way we feel about things is what motivates our actions and accomplishes our development. You have learned a great deal about yourself and you have come to respect your own abilities. These abilities are part of a long pattern of development which has brought you to where you are now. These are qualities developed in previous incarnations and are so much a part of you that you couldn't live without them. These abilities are available to you now. At this moment you are realizing a potential which is coming into fruition, a potential which existed when you were created. Everything you are is now present in this moment. Now is when we can do anything we want to do because now is the point of power. Everything that happens, happens in the now, and anything can be changed now by changing our beliefs and attitudes now.

You are wondering where God and His plan and His power come into this. The fact that now is the point of power and that we change through our beliefs is a concept of God. God willed all that happens in this original concept of life. What seems to be our power in the pres-

159

ent is simply God's power in the All in All! We, as tiny
atoms of God, are functioning, which is God's plan, and
the manner in which we function is our contribution to
the plan. By using our power in the present constructively, we are fulfilling our part in this great drama
of life. When we fail to do our part, we are prompted and
encouraged to see clearly. Now is all there is. It is the
time for change, for action. It is powerful. We can change
anything now, not tomorrow, not yesterday, but now.
Right here and now everything is all right. Tomorrow
never comes, and yesterday is over. Now we can always
cope. Now is the action of faith.

Bringing now down to a fine point, we realize that we
have what we need, and if we want what we need, we
have what we want too. There are no problems that
cannot be solved. The solution to any problem is always
present within the problem itself. Fear never deals with
the moment. It anticipates without knowing the solution. You know that although you have experienced a
great many hardships, you have never had to experience
more than you could cope with. This is the way it is.
Even if we can't see the future, we know that the present
is okay. When tomorrow becomes now, it will be okay
too. There is no reason to worry, but you seem to find
time to do so anyway. It is important to think this
through and cope with it.

*I guess my biggest problem is insecurity. I know I
shouldn't feel this way, but I do.*

Let us examine the true nature of what you call insecurity. What you are feeling is the result of changing circumstances. Circumstances are always changing, and
events reflect the change. The only way to combat insecurity is to look around and ask whether everything is
all right now. If the answer is yes, you must realize that

Insecurity

your life is always just now, and if you are all right now,
that is proof that it is always all right. What happens
tomorrow won't happen until tomorrow, and at that
time it will be now and you will be able to cope. There is
nothing about the present moment to cause insecurity.
Insecurity comes from not living in the moment. This is
the crux of the problem. If you accept and act upon what
I tell you, you will be able to rid yourself of these negative
feelings.

The events of tomorrow are affected by the decisions
and actions of today. The mire you have been through in
recent years is proof that you get what you project. If we
project fear and emotionalism, we will get events which
foster fear and emotionalism. Living constructively in
the moment, our projects are both constructive and
immediate and therefore eternal in nature. This is the
secret to success in living, and the most we can expect
from ourselves. You must utilize now or our work will
lag. Keep your mind on what you are doing and make
sure it is constructive. Procrastination is a hindrance to
progress. Now is golden. It offers endless opportunity. It
is always with us, but we often don't heed it.

The value of concentration must not be overlooked.
This involves the use of now. The reason you have had
trouble concentrating is that your mind has wanted to
involve itself with everything going on around you. It
must be put to work in useful ways as a secretary. No
good executive is run by a secretary. Neither should you
be run by your mind. Always try to be single-purposed in
the now, not involved with several thoughts and reactions at once. When you do this work with me, your one
activity is to listen, nothing else. Don't try to decipher
what you receive and anticipate what you think you
should be hearing. Concentrate on the single process of
listening, and you will indeed hear what I have to say.

This is the way to live each moment, concentrating on what we are doing in that moment, not dispersing it. We must set aside time for all importances, learn to schedule our time, and follow through. Now is always the time of action and reaction. Now is always when events both active and passive occur. Now is always the time to change our minds and so change our lives. There is a reason why people say, "If you want to get something done, give it to a busy person." Such a person has learned how to schedule his life and concentrate on importances now. True accomplishment is dependent upon concentration, on construction now. Your only problem with communication now is lack of concentration. Without concentration, lethargy sets in and you tend to fall asleep. If you keep concentrated, you will find the vitality you need for any and all tasks. Don't let your mind wander. If this is allowed to happen, the energy becomes dispersed and your hearing will falter. It is better to stop and wait awhile when this happens than to continue with no concentration or energy. Your only activity now is listening to me. This is all I expect from you. No other startling feats are necessary to get this work done. Your ability to hear me is well developed now, so now we can do all we've set out to do.

Time, space, and motion are all elements of the same thing—function. Your present depends upon your past only to the extent that your past was expressed in the present. Your past doesn't exist now. It existed in the present once. The function which takes place in time, space, and motion exists only in the present. Without function, there is no time, space, and motion to refer to. To recall the past is to recall function, at which time it all exists in the present. Thoughts are things. Function can exist in the mind. Time, space, and motion can be creations in the mind with the creation of function past and future. All that exists, exists in the present. The past doesn't exist except when it is re-created in the mind, at which point it exists in the present. When you travel from point A to point B, points A and B remain the same. The time, space, and motion involved in the traveling exist because of the function of traveling. When you think back to point A when arriving at point B, you are re-creating and bringing into existence a function which exists only in your mind, and there it exists in the present. Your mind and your body can be functioning in two different circumstances at the same time and both in the present. Think about this.

God the Father-Mother

I'd been told that God the Father was the
most satisfactory concept we could have, but
I thought of the Eastern concept of God the
Mother and felt the need for a clarification.

*I'm still not sure why we need to describe God, the All
in All, in limited terms.*

The word "God," whatever it is in any language, has
served all people to express man's understanding and
acknowledgment of a supreme Being Who is all-loving
and all-powerful, creator of life and the soul of goodness.
He is our Father, benevolent and wanting perfection for
us, His creation. This supreme Being is indeed the All in
All. He is all of everything that exists and certainly all of
personality. So we come back to the concept of a personal God, our Father, which is as valid a concept, even
if fragmented, as any other available. Does the concept
of the All in All, Supreme Good, Mind, or whatever, tell
us any more about the true nature of God than the word
of God, with Jesus' reference to the Father as in the
Lord's Prayer ("Our Father . . .")? I think not, and I
believe that the one attribute of God to which all of us,
Christians and non-Christians alike, can relate as people is the personal concept of a loving Father Who wants
ultimate perfection for all of His creatures, and to accomplish this He is willing to expose them to anything
which will bring about growth. All events point to construction as the ultimate purpose because this is God's

165

will. Love is the motivation of God's actions, and love must be our response to Him. To think of Him as our Father is to relate personally to the cause of all being, the All in All. Christ brought this concept to the world and rightly so, since it provides the personal, intimate relationship that all Christians share.

We here see the picture somewhat differently. We are always aware of a presence which is benevolent and loving. The appearance of the perfect ones is always an awesome experience. The quality of peace and love which emanates from the beam of light that pervades this world provides us with all the food we ever need. The presence of God is felt here quite literally. The feeling is of a loving Parent and we are His children, sharing the sheer ecstasy of His presence. Great benefit is derived from thinking of God as Father, because although Christ is as complete an embodiment of God as Christians know, each of us, to whatever degree we have grown as children of God, is also an embodiment of God, meant in the long run to share His state of being. This we must earn by living our lives according to His will for us. God the Father is a perfect example of concept fitting need. Human beings must relate to their source in a human, personal way in order to understand themselves and their surroundings. God is not going to do anything which a loving father would not do.

You are wondering whether it is possible to think of God as Mother. The answer is yes. The totality which is God must encompass both male and female concepts. You think that if you think of God as Father you are denying God the Mother. I will say this: it took a father and a mother to create you in your present state, but this is only procreation. Creation is achieved by one individual entity, God. God required no one else to produce life. There is nothing sexual involved in creation.

All elements are present in God, Father and Mother elements alike. The two polarities, positive and negative, active and passive, are essential in life. The two opposites must be present in all creation, all mutation, all development of life forms. To create life, God possesses both negative and positive values. The purpose of all creation is perfection. In the process of living, we experience each of the essential elements, active and passive, positive and negative, during different incarnations. This translates into male and female.

Every living creature needs maleness and femaleness in order to procreate and/or experience the qualities of both sexual states during various incarnations. By the time we develop beyond the reincarnational cycle, we possess both elements to a great degree, and you can be sure that the state of perfection will contain both elements fully. There are male and female qualities in all human beings, even though one is dominant in any given incarnation. Sexuality as such is needed only during an incarnation. Active and passive, positive and negative, however, are present in all, incarnate and discarnate alike.

We could say God the Father-Mother or God the Positive-Negative and be saying the same truth in different ways. However, God the Father or God the Mother fulfills the same human need. God is our creator and is intimately involved in our development. We could become so overpowered by the magnitude of the concept of God that we might overlook the extreme care with which He considers each and every element in His creation. "Are not two sparrows sold for a farthing? and one of them shall not fall on the ground without your Father" (Matthew 10:29). Think this over. Most people are a mixture of values, both active and passive, because they have lived so many lives as both male and female and are preparing for that state of balance which has to do with final objective. We should learn quickly from this that there can be no single concept of God which truly describes all there is. All we can do is try to bring our thoughts of God as close to ourselves as possible.

Our parents are our most intimate authority figures, and it follows that parental love is the closest thing we know to God's love for us. Therefore, to conceive of God as Father or Mother, or Father-Mother, brings us closer to Him in human terms than any other concept could. When Christ said to pray by saying, "Our Father . . ." he knew what he was doing. He was bringing an understanding of love.

Truth and Tolerance

One morning Richard started our communication by saying he thought I took
everything too literally. Truth and con-
ceptions of truth, he said, are quite different
matters.

*How can I know whether I am understanding cor-
rectly?*

Don't try to be too literal in your interpretation of what I
say. These concepts are intended to move your feeling,
to stir your inner self and allow you to recognize the
truth which lies within. As concepts they are subject to
many interpretations, depending upon the place from
which they are seen. Our stage of development determines our understanding, and while all interpretations of a truth have validity, a truth remains a
truth. No matter what we think about it, the fact itself
doesn't change. A narrow point of view can be true as far
as it goes, but the more developed person will adopt a
broader attitude toward the matter just because he has
broader vision. Intolerance is negative and doesn't allow
for the possibility of other interpretations of truth. The
more developed we become, the broader our vision and
the greater our tolerance for other attitudes.

Tolerance should be extended to all of our relationships. Practice what you preach and try to be what
you want from others. Tolerance allows us to recognize
that all of us are traveling the same route. Some ride in

limousines, some run, some just crawl along, and others hobble, but we're all on the same road. Truth and tolerance are related only to the degree to which we see the truth. The tolerant person sees the truth through a broader spectrum than the intolerant person. The truth is never altered; it remains the same truth no matter how many different ways it is perceived.

Don't stray from the conviction that we play to win. The atmosphere we create around us is very important to the success of our life experiences. Whether our problems are physical, mental, psychological, or spiritual, they must be surrounded by construction, and the winning attitude creates the proper conditions for the breeding of a beneficial outcome to any circumstance. If we play to win, we are using faith and hope, two of the essentials to constructive living. And if we add love for those within our sphere of influence, we have all of the ingredients for success. Development is our goal, and success must be seen in that light. If we play to win, we must be willing to play by the rules and accept the outcome as fair. This is the way we learn to be good sports and enter each contest with optimism, knowing that there are no losers really, since every event can be turned to good.

The happy and optimistic person is one who has learned a great lesson from living, a gift from God as a reward for his efforts. The purpose of life is to develop to a state of perfection. Truth is the state of perfection. Truth is the only state which is perfect. Truth, then, is to be sought by all those who are consciously seeking growth toward perfection. Growth is a matter of relationships. We learn, grow, and develop through our relationships. God works through people in both the incarnate and discarnate worlds.

If you wonder who you really are, sit down and outline

in your mind all of the events of your life to see just where they have led you. You can see how the opportunities developed and what you did about them. The line of events will lead you directly to where you are. Where you are is a direct result of the way you have reacted to the events of your life. Who we are, then, bears a direct relationship to where we are. We are where we are because of who we are. Our potential is quite different. It is what we can become if our reactions to the events of our lives are constructive. Our own sense of truth is a helpful guide in determining the purpose of events. This is part of our spiritual equipment and must be used when we are working through the plan of our lives, of which the events are guideposts. Accepting events as purposeful and constructive at the core requires us to use our sense of truth, along with intuition and love, to determine the direction in which the events are leading us.

The person who sees truly is tolerant of others for two reasons. First, everyone must learn from his own mistakes, and being judgmental of others only reflects upon our own problems. Second, no one can truly see the inner life and turmoil being experienced by another, so we have no basis for making judgments of others' actions. We certainly can be aware of people's problems, but the truth about them lies hidden deep within and can be understood only by them. Outward appearances do not necessarily reflect the inner condition, although some behavior patterns are indicative of certain conditions which are shared by us all. One may, then, deduce certain problems which affect another, but his total situation is far too complex for anyone but himself to understand. Tolerance is an expression of love, the epitome of which is creative harmony. Negative thinking has no place in growth. The truth is always shaded by negative, deterrent thought.

The moment must be truly realized if we are to live according to God's will. The moment itself contains the energy needed to function fully. We can always cope with the moment if we concentrate on it fully. Open your hearts to the moment, give it all you have, and you will learn to see truly. Truth is constant. It never changes. It can be seen from many angles, and from each vantage point it appears different. But this is only the way it is perceived. It is not the way it is. Our aim is to reach a high enough point of achievement that we may be able to see it straight on, not obliquely. To comprehend truth fully, one must reach perfection. The way to understand it is by striving. The effort makes the difference. If we are ready to understand, we will understand. He who achieves understanding has worked for it. There is no other way. Effort is required, and the more we apply it to the task at hand, the more we become achievers. Spiritual growth must be earned, and this means tackling those things which are very hard to do and trying with all of our might to move them forward and to move forward through them.

The truth is so much a part of life that it is difficult to separate the two. Life contains the elements of truth, and truth exists in all of life. God decided to create life because He wanted truth to abound in multiplicity. To be true to ourselves is to recognize our origin and our potential. Living life truly is living according to God's will, striving to accomplish the ultimate goal we have all been promised, unique at-oneness with Him and unique individuality as well, the ultimate truth expressed. Life has the potential of expressing truth perfectly. To say we think an idea is true is to say that it could be false. This depends upon our perception of truth. Truth remains so no matter what we think about it. Our opinion of whether or not it is so is not the issue.

The issue really is whether or not we recognize the truth as such. If we can see clearly, we can recognize truth. Understanding is the reward we receive for effort, effort to learn who we are and why we are here and what we should be doing. These fundamental questions form the basis for understanding life and, ultimately, truth. If we question the truth of the thoughts and statements of others, we are putting ourselves in the seat of God, an act of pride unworthy of the novitiate. God does not question; He knows. If we recognize that someone else is not seeing clearly, we are not being judgmental, merely tolerant, accepting the fact that we all have deficiencies until we reach our ultimate goal, and then there is no need for opinion at all.

We live in a total state of truth. "Live and let live" is a better attitude than wanting to save the world from all its sins. One who presumes to judge another by his own standards is not seeing clearly. What is right for one may very well be wrong for another. Only the individual can know about his or her own needs and desires. No one can make true judgments about another. If we judge according to our own standards, we miss the truth involved.

The value of understanding cannot be overstressed. The more we work to eliminate our own problems, the more we recognize the growth in others. Our heart feelings about the circumstances of our lives are to be trusted over our head feelings. The brain is an efficient worker, but it does not originate conditions; it functions within them. Our heart feelings come closer to the truth, the constructive element which lies within the circumstances and culminating events of life. Follow your heart and you will always be close to the truth. Truth is the essence of God's Being and therefore the essence of all being. Truth encompasses God's will (construction) and God's love (creative harmony). The purpose of events for all is the realization of truth. With each event we reap the consequences of the circumstances which brought it about. Since we contribute to those circumstances through our reactions to previous events, we are continually presented with the possibility of understanding the truth about consequences. To the extent to which we are responsible, we contribute either to construction or deterrence. The understanding and acceptance of this fact enable us to see truly and act accordingly. The realization of truth, then, builds character, fosters spiritual growth, and aligns us on the side of construction and harmony.

Fear

With all I had learned and all my efforts to see clearly, I found that I continued to worry endlessly.

How can I conquer fear?

Fear plays a large part in our thoughts and beliefs. When we worry about a situation, we allow fear to dominate our thoughts, and the emotions which result are all deterrent. Fear is never a part of clear thinking. Our Father loves us and wants us to learn. Everything that happens has a constructive base. Death is nothing to fear, and calamity, poverty, and pain can be dealt with when they are upon us. Fear doesn't cope with reality, but anticipates a future which, in all likelihood, won't even occur. If it does, the moment brings with it the solution to the problem. There is nothing to fear but fear itself. Don't allow yourself to become victimized by it. It has no place in a constructive life. Fear is an expression of insecurity. Insecurity is part of the makeup of those who experience fear. Fear is not grounded in reality. It is a fantasy stemming from insecurity and pride. Insecurity is a manifestation of pride. Pride is a basic human fault. It is a blinding factor in human relationships. It manifests itself in so many ways and masks its nature in so many ways that it becomes very difficult to understand and eliminate. Where there is true humility, there is faith and trust and no pride. Without humility we can never understand our kinship with our Maker.

Fear, then, stems from pride and can be eliminated only through humility. To be like God we must have experienced and mastered all those elements which deter growth. Being constructive, we also have the capability of being deterrent. The choice makes the difference. A fearful person is often one who has a need to feel superior. This stems from a deep-seated insecurity which must be covered up at all costs. One of the costs is fear. The insecurity disguises itself in this manner and is free to express itself without recognition. Fear becomes an uncontrollable result of pride. In order to eliminate the fear we must root out pride and get down to the basic insecurity. The knowledge of our true nature helps to bring about an understanding of our faults and thereby eliminate them. Also, God has provided fear with a constructive side. An individual who never allows himself to see things as they are, but lives in a world of unreality, can be shocked into looking at reality through fear. It may take such an emotion to shake him up and bring him to his senses. In this way, fear can bring the pride and the insecurity from which it stems to the surface, where it can be recognized and examined for what it is. It is possible to learn and grow from the experience of fear.

Fear can also be the impetus which removes us from an intolerable situation in a hurry. It can free us from compulsive, deterrent acts. The fear of being caught can often cause us to run from acts to which we are compelled. These moments become moments of clarity which can start us down the constructive path. Fear, then, is essential to the human condition. We know that fear is often a manifestation of pride, but we haven't discussed the essential quality of fear. Without fear we would never learn to see clearly. The need for us to learn our lessons implies that we do so because we fear the consequences if we don't. It is said that fear is the better part of valor. This merely proves the law of cause and effect. Our experiences can teach us to seek change, because we fear the repetition which will follow if we don't. However, the nature of fear depends entirely on its source. It is an outward manifestation of an inner condition, and its value depends on its source. You know that the most devastating events of your life have been the instruments of your greatest benefit. Day-to-day vicissitudes are necessary, but it is the major events which bring about the most fundamental changes. If we can accept them as opportunities, we will take leaps ahead in our understanding and spiritual growth.

It is the rare soul who can see clearly in the midst of calamity, but time allows us the necessary perspective in our search for truth. Fear must be put into perspective. If we fear that which doesn't exist, if we fear the future, if we fear what might happen, our fears are groundless and stem from deterrence. If we fear our present circumstances, maybe we are being prompted to change them, to remove ourselves from them and take an action which will alleviate them. Such fear can be constructive because it brings us to grips with conditions which need change.

Intellect and Growth

One day, I was thinking of the concept of a life plan and how it is affected by reactions to events. Out of my puzzlement came the next question.

If my reaction affects the outcome of the events of my life, isn't my life plan at the mercy of my understanding?

Can a life plan possibly succeed without understanding? The answer is yes. When you say "understanding," I assume you mean specific knowledge such as you have. You don't need to know anything specific. All that is needed for an incarnation to succeed is a constructive attitude. Those who look upon life negatively are always presented with problems to solve. The solution is contained in the problems they are given to solve. We must be brought around to an understanding of how to react to events. If we suffer enough in this way, we may finally come to realize that a change of attitude could help. It often takes extreme adversity to accomplish this.

The intellect is only as valuable as the construction it brings about. To be bright and intelligent is not enough. These faculties must be applied to good. Growth is not dependent either upon intellect or knowledge, but rather on seeing simply and clearly and acting constructively. Each incarnation carries with it the necessary ingredients for certain accomplishments, and intellect is included in these ingredients. It is not what we have but how we use what we have that matters. The

179

simplest soul may accomplish the most during an incarnation by going about his daily tasks with simple desire to do right by others and therefore by himself. We all need a conscious alignment with construction, at whatever level we find ourselves.

You are thinking that it is probably better to be good than bright. This is certainly true. However, we must realize that the elements of development are designed for individual growth, so our mental capacity is part of an individual plan for spiritual development. We cannot compare goodness to intelligence. Goodness, or qualities of any nature, good or bad, are what we bring with us to an incarnation. Intelligence, on any level, is what we are given as an element of our development in any incarnation. It is a part of the circumstances which result from our choice of parents. We grow during an incarnation through the pursuit and satisfaction of our inner feelings and desires, within the circumstances of our lives. The intelligence we have in any given incarnation is just right for the job. Goodness is either something we are working for or something we bring with us when we come. Growth is the achievement of any quality we may need with the means at hand. Those who achieve much may not necessarily be sweet, kind, generous, and loving. They may be none of those things. But if, in the process of living, they acquire a quality essential to their specific needs, they have grown and developed according to plan.

Think about what it is which makes the difference in an individual life experience. Think of what living out an incarnation successfully really means. What counts the most in the long run? The most important accomplishment one can make in an incarnation is to understand oneself and one's needs and desires and to follow them. Everything else aside, if we do this, we will be true to ourselves, we will be accomplishing our purpose, and we will be living constructive lives following God's will. Everyone's condition is unique. Don't spend time wishing you were someone else. Rather, spend your time probing your inner feelings so you can learn who *you* are and why you are where you are. Develop your talents so you can have a functioning skill to get along with in the world.

Does negative thought really affect the plan of a life?
Yes, negative thinking does affect the plan of a life; it alters the plan to achieve the resultant need, understanding. There is always the opportunity to get back on track and proceed, if not on schedule, at least in the right direction. The plan of a life is a plan of goals. It is involved with intent, not event. Specific events are the fruition of specific circumstances. The input into circumstances comes from various sources, partly established by the choice of parents and partly contributed by reactions to events. The culmination of a set of circumstances into an event marks the end of one set of circumstances and the beginning of another. Since the intent of an incarnation is construction, it is from this standpoint that circumstances develop. If a reaction to an event is deterrent, the ensuing circumstances, no matter how they may appear, are the result of the need which the reaction brought about. If we haven't yet learned what kind of reaction results in growth, we are presented with another opportunity to learn through another set of circumstances to fit the need. Things are not what they seem. Construction always dominates a situation, whether or not it appears so. The need for growth is satisfied by all events, through one means or another. Circumstances are basically constructive. We find the answer to the puzzle of life by examining our heart feelings to understand ourselves and our true needs. Then and only then will we be able to understand

what really has been happening to us and what our
thinking has done to us. This moment of self-realization
is all that is needed to alter the direction of a life completely. This is why it is so important to know and trust
and love ourselves. Without faith and hope we are
blinded to the clear vision we can receive from our spiritual equipment (love, sense of truth, and intuition).
"Know thyself" is the admonition which must be heeded
by all who want to progress. Those who hate themselves,
who think of themselves in negative terms, are not probing their inner being deeply enough, are not seeing the
worth which lies hidden, their true selves. Instead, they
accept the manifestations of their karmic problems as
their real selves and find what they observe unaccept-
able. They lump them all together with their compulsions and run to the intellect, which cannot compete
with compulsion, to solve their problems.

***Why can't intellect, which we regard so highly these
days, compete with compulsion?***

Intellect is a tool, a much-needed tool, but a tool
nonetheless. It is not a part of the eternal being. It is part
of the circumstances of a life during a specific incarnation. It is not part of the equipment we have been given
to solve our spiritual problems. As you know, our spiritual equipment is love, sense of truth, and intuition.
Intellect is intended not to be used to solve spiritual
problems, but rather to cope with day-to-day vicissitudes. Compulsion is the manifestation of an acquired
fault, a part of the eternal being. It must be overcome
through the use of spiritual equipment. Intuition, the
intellect of the eternal being, is much more capable of
handling compulsion. But the sense of truth must be
brought into play in order to get down to the basic fault,
of which the compulsion is merely a manifestation. It is
necessary to know ourselves in order to solve our problems.

Daydreams and Imagination

Is there a connection between imagination and heart feelings?

Looking beneath the surface, we find a world of dreams, hope, expectation, and desire which can lead us to our ultimate goal. The channel is the circumstances of our lives lived constructively. Daydreaming can be a very productive occupation. It can do two things: (1) divert our attention from deterrent thought and emotion and (2) create beneficial circumstances. The child who daydreams is escaping from reality, but in so doing is creating an alternate reality which can be helpful to his development. Sexual daydreams often prevent overt acts which could cause harm to the spirit. Dreaming up our future is a positive act and suggests good possibilities. By setting aside time to bring our dreams into the present (now), we give them reality. This should be a regular isolated experience. When daydreams stem from true heart feelings, they become expressions of the eternal being based on stored-up knowledge. Imagination and dreams are bridges to our world. They can be constructive in coping with life's pressures. If we let ourselves go and dream up the perfect life for us, it enables us to build a strong base of operation in our daily lives.

The reality of dreams cannot be overestimated. Everything we dream about has reality. The dreaming gives it reality. Dreams of a perfect life represent potential, and if we work to bring these dreams about, we will indeed be developing the qualities we have come to achieve. We are talking about the kinds of dreams which lie deep within us, the ones we are afraid to expose to the world for fear

183

of being ridiculed, the dreams which move us to tears when we bring ourselves to think of them. Dreams of wealth, sensuality, and the like, are peripheral and not a part of our heart's dreams. The potential for growth which is expressed through daydreams lies deep within our souls. This is the potential we want to make a permanent part of our being. This is why we are where we are. Our job is to trust these feelings and allow them to lead us onto a constructive path.

One way to learn about ourselves is to explore our dreams and hopes. These are the stuff of which accomplishment is made. Those who allow themselves to be swayed by peer pressure to the detriment of their dreams and hopes are those who will lose their way. There is no substitute for what our hearts tell us, because that is the source of our being. You can help both yourself and others by imagining that we are all part of a unified whole joined in love and destined to become perfect. When we picture the perfect state, it makes no difference whether or not our imagining is based on fact. Our dreams become real through the dreaming. What we will finally experience in the perfect state will be the ultimate fulfillment of our potential and the ultimate result of our own efforts. Our dreams and imagination contribute to the ultimate state. The outcome of the plan, then, depends upon us. If we are willing to know ourselves, we will learn much that will not be apparent to others. But since we alone are responsible for ourselves, our job is not to go out seeking our fortune, but rather to seek the knowledge of truth from within. We are worthy of every effort we make to understand ourselves. We have the equipment we need to move on. It's up to us.

Communication

I wondered if communication between the incarnate and discarnate states was developing throughout the world.

Does communication have widespread significance?

Communication is a very important part of God's plan. The present age is filled with people who have developed the ability to communicate directly, and they are beginning to make inroads in understanding. This ability is latent within all human beings and was an integral part of early man's equipment. Because early man was aware of his inner vision, the curtain between the two worlds was not drawn and psychic events were not regarded as remarkable. Physical and mental development brought with it the worship of physical and mental prowess to the detriment of psychic ability. The conviction developed that the rational person used his brain, while the irrational person trusted his intuition. Reality was what we saw around us, and inner vision was a figment of the imagination. Those who heard voices from within were deranged. This development of self-will brought down the curtain between the worlds, and only now are we able to say that conditions are beginning to change.

What about indirect communication, through guardian angels, for example?

You are wondering just how important this is to development. I'll say this: All people are being helped from this side, whether they know it or not. Even for those whom

185

it is impossible to get through to, every effort is made. The development of everyone on earth is monitored by someone in the Place of Preparation, and whenever possible, assistance is given in the form of thought transferral, mental suggestion, and brain impingement. Everybody has at least one person whose job it is to help.

The Spirit

I felt the need to know more about the nature
of the spirit within us.

*Will you clarify my understanding of the eternal be-
ing, the spirit?*

The spirit is the element in us which is seeking perfection. Our free will allows us either to strive for betterment or to give in to wrongdoing. Our spirit is our
saving victim—the God element in us, who suffers from
our ego-centered compulsions, but who is the key to our
salvation. The spirit is our basic, fundamental self, the
self that yearns for perfection, the self that has put its
trust in our ability to see clearly enough to follow the
path of construction to its ultimate end. There are two of
us. The eternal being who lives in our hearts already
knows what he wants and is cognizant of the circumstances which are necessary to achieve it. The temporal
being, the person of this incarnation, is required to
experience the entire gamut of life from birth to death,
and during that process of physical development he
must learn also who he is, why he is where he is, and
what he must do about it. Growth is the essence of life,
and spiritual understanding must be relearned during
each incarnation. True, each time we return we are
differently equipped, depending upon what we have acquired from past experience, but nevertheless the veil
can be lifted by our efforts only. The realization of who
we are must be relearned each time. Developed souls

have little difficulty with this, primarily because of the absence of deterrence, which blocks vision. The spirit is ever-present and available. This eternal being can advise only in response to queries from the temporal being. If the temporal being initiates the question and the question is from heart, the eternal being, who resides in the heart, will surely answer clearly and truthfully. The spirit, the inner voice, the Holy Ghost of Christian teaching, and the "God within" of Eastern thought are all the same, the voice of the eternal being. We are all segments of God and privy to truth, but it lies buried within our heart and must be uncovered through effort. The effort brings the growth. Without effort there would be no growth. The spirit dwells in the heart; therefore, heart feelings are clues to the desires of the spirit. By utilizing our spiritual equipment, we uncover the desires of the spirit and come to see what our true heart feelings are.

Effort

Is there no growth without effort?

The only way to learn is to try. The effort is always worth the price. Construction is the result of effort. Effort is basic to all growth. It is often true that the effort is more important than the result, because effort is the foundation on which we construct our very beings. On our side there is nothing but emptiness for the new arrivals who have never really tried. They have created nothing to rely on when they find themselves alone in a strange country with no luggage! Effort helps to develop understanding in daily life. We must grasp what is meant by effort. Our bodies are making effort in so many ways it is impossible to grasp. Our spirit made the effort to bring us into being here and now. Our job here involves effort from the moment we wake in the morning until we go to bed at night. Desire and energy contribute to its functioning.

Since effort is so basic to the design of living, it is important to recognize the difference between constructive and deterrent effort. Effort goes into deterrence as well as construction, so we should always try to make it count for something by being sure we are functioning constructively. Effort is the essence of life. The goal of life is perfection, and effort is the means by which it is achieved. There is no such thing as worthless effort. The person who puts effort to deterrence is speeding along toward events from which he could learn and come to see more clearly. The person who puts effort toward construction is doing the will of God. The person who is unwilling, out of fear, self-satisfaction, or just plain indolence, to make any effort at all is the one who will end up in deep trouble.

There is no time when effort can be discounted. Energy is required in the process of making effort. Those who are low in energy are usually those who never make the effort to do what they should. Those who are afraid of the heart feelings are really fearful of failure. This is a manifestation of the most insidious of all faults, pride. We might say that many people make enormous effort because of pride, and we might ask whether that, too, isn't wrong. Prideful effort will lead to events which clearly are lessons to be learned. "Pride goeth before a fall" is true enough, but the greater the effort, the harder the fall and the greater the opportunity to learn. The smaller the effort, the less the reaction and the less clear the resultant lesson to be learned.

Those who make minimal effort just to stay alive, for whatever reasons, usually muddle through life as if in a maze, never finding their way out. Such people are allowing their karmic problems to assume supremacy over their heart feelings and never learn who they are, why they are where they are, and what they have to do—a pitiful, wasted incarnation.

Beliefs

I realized that we all have different beliefs in
life and wondered how they might affect our
development.

What is the purpose of beliefs?
The plan of life, as it has been laid down to you, is the
plan of God's dream now. What will come does not concern us, because only when it happens can we grasp and
face it. What has happened in the past does not concern
us, because we are the product of the past, working hard
to achieve our goals in the present. The present is all
there is for anyone. We know that God is All in All and
that we, and all living matter, are incomplete fragments
of God, gradually working our way toward becoming
whole and filling our rightful niche in the plan of perfection for all. We know that we are helped at every turn but
that our own efforts are of utmost importance, since
individual realization can only come from individual
effort. To become uniquely individual and uniquely at-
one with God is a joint effort of God and all His members.
This dream can be realized only if we are willing to do our
share.

The privilege of becoming implies the responsibility to
become. We know that everyone has a special place in
this plan which can be filled by no one else. The success
of the whole requires the success of each and every part.
We know that everything we are going through is for one
purpose alone—to give us understanding so we can act
constructively at every opportunity. We know that our

191

own lives are special and that every special quality is needed to complete the plan. We know that our own concerns are important to our development and that everyone must recognize his own uniqueness and value to God's plan. We know that we are doing our jobs the best way we know how and that that is all we can hope to do for our own development. We know that obedience and dedication to construction (God's will) as a way of life are all there is to achievement, and that the one who travels the constructive path will inevitably succeed in reaching the final goal. We know there are many mysteries we do not comprehend, but we also are sure that all will be revealed in the end to him who lives with faith in the goodness of God.

The only purpose of beliefs is growth. Many have beliefs which don't allow for growth, but so it is. If what we believe is deterrent, we will cause ourselves great difficulty. Since what we believe today is the cause of what we do tomorrow, our beliefs have a powerful hold on us and our development. As you believe, so you are—this is certainly true. We may give lip service to lofty ideals, but it is what we believe that motivates our actions.

Try now to organize your thoughts. What do you really believe? Do you believe you can get ahead while wasting time? Do you believe your destiny is predetermined no matter what you do? Do you believe your problems are over? Do you believe everything works out for the best even if you don't do your part? If you believe any or all of these statements, you are in for trouble. God's grace is only as active as we are constructive. It is the law of parallels. We receive in kind, but more so.

Are you saying if I act deterrently, I receive deterrence as well?

Yes, exactly. We get what we give. Giving and receiving are the same act. If we give construction, we receive construction. If we give deterrence, we receive deterrence. It is like a magnet. If we are negative, we attract negativism. It is much harder to get back on the track than to stay on it. One little variation in our response to the plan of our lives, one little regression, brings down upon us all of the regressive elements we have been working to eliminate.

Try to see things now as they really are. You are wondering where your beliefs will lead you. They are only valuable if they are put into practice. If we really believe that our will and God's will are one, we surely must know that what we want is what we get. The best possible way to live is to see this point clearly and respond to it constructively. There is nothing we need that we don't have. What we want should be what we need, because what we need will surely be what we get. Beliefs are the groundwork upon which our lives are built, and they affect our reactions to the events of our lives. If we want what we need, we will want what we get. But beneath all of this there must be the belief that everything we get has a constructive basis from which an important lesson can be learned. Here again, it is necessary to return to the essential belief in the goodness of God and His design for growth for us all. When we know that everything that happens to us is for the good, we are accepting the most basic principle of life—love. Events in themselves are benign and become deterrent only by the reactions of those involved. If we believe this, we recognize that the purpose of life is growth, and our beliefs will move us forward. The manner in which we are propelled forward depends upon the nature of our beliefs. If we believe that now is all we have and that if we live each moment as constructively as possible now, building one moment upon the other, we are surely living according to God's will for us and will realize the most from each incarnation.

Please explain the difference between believing that I am well and accepting things as they are.

The way things are is the way things should be. If you feel well, then you can surely believe your feelings, and that's the way things are at the moment. You don't need the doctor to tell you whether you're well or not. What the doctor is doing is caring for your problems for you. The way we feel is affected to a great degree by what we believe. As you well know, all experiences are valuable, and only those who experience them can see them for what they really are. If we are sure that what we get is what we want, we will always feel right about things, no matter what the appearances are.

Keep your mind clear about the moment. If you believe this moment represents eternity, that eternity is made up of moment-to-moment reality, you are indeed living in the manner you should and will realize the most from it. If you believe in the need to live each moment constructively, your belief will affect the outcome of your efforts. The reason for living is development. Development is constructive, and construction is the nature of God's will. So by living constructively, moment to moment, we are fusing our will to the will of God and are developing according to plan. The nature of the will of God is construction. The nature of the love of God is creative harmony. If we believe this, and live our own lives accordingly, we are living our beliefs as God does, being true to our nature as atoms of Him.

That's easier said than done!

True. But we must have goals to work for, or our progress would be deterred, and this is the one intolerable situation in life. All circumstances and events further progress and development one way or another. Whenever our reaction creates deterrence, the circumstances and events which ensue are automatically altered to get us back on track by forcing us to see more clearly, by causing us to endure consequences which could open our eyes to truth. Development is essential to our being, and nothing, I repeat, nothing is allowed to deter it for long. Those who learn the lessons of life move forward and are rewarded for their efforts. Those who do not must continue to be taught until they finally come around to seeing things as they really are. There is no better way to learn than through our mistakes. The one thing which proves out a belief is the outcome of acting on it. If we want to be sure our beliefs are constructive, we will be able to tell by observing the outcome of putting them into practice.

Is there a required rate of progress in an incarnation, and does it depend upon the plan which has been previously set?

Yes and no. By yes, I mean the plan of a life is set in advance. But that plan always represents difficulties to be overcome and qualities to be acquired. No one comes with objectives so minute and qualities so developed that no effort need be made to accomplish them. People who appear to live lives with no strain or effort, who protect themselves from their surroundings, who have no struggle to survive, and whose ambitions are strictly limited may not seem to have given themselves much to do this time. This conclusion could be wrong. Such people might not have utilized the circumstances of their lives, but settled back into the very condition they have come to overcome. The situation is not so very different from that of the compulsive, self-indulgent nature, finding itself succumbing to the faults it most wants to eliminate. Appearances are deceptive because we never really know what is going on inside another person. But, in any case, don't envy the easygoing, affluent man with no apparent problems. You can be sure his real problems are there, whether or not he is coping with them. No one on earth is without problems. The earth is the battleground for conquering them.

Believe me when I say we are all here for growth through learning and that we need each other in order to solve our own problems. The richest person is the one who serves his neighbors to the best of his ability and himself in the process. Believe in your own capabilities and you will recognize your kinship to all living things. We humans are all imperfect atoms of God's making, struggling to become perfect through our own efforts even as He is perfect.

Summary of Truths

Here, at Richard's request, I am listing the truths I have come to believe in as a result of his teaching.

1. Immortality is a reality.
2. Reincarnation is a fact.
3. We are here because we want to be here.
4. The circumstances of our lives have been chosen by us as the best for our development.
5. Each incarnation has a goal, a purpose.
6. We must learn who we are and why we are here. Our true heart feelings are the source.
7. Our talents show us the way.
8. Our job is to live each day constructively in harmony with others.
9. Our concerns must lie within our immediate sphere of influence only.
10. The qualities we have acquired in the Place of Preparation are given quantity through the living out of an incarnation and thereby become permanent.
11. As children of God we are granted free will, which offers us the opportunity to choose either God's will (construction) or self-will (deterrence).
12. Free will allows us the opportunity to reach perfection.
13. Construction (God's will) always wins out in the long run.
14. The power of the negative force is not destructive, merely deterrent.
15. Construction lies within every event no matter how

it appears. Our job is to see the construction and follow its teaching.

16. Our final goal is the perfect state, at-one with God and yet uniquely individual.

17. Love is the guiding power which fuses all of life into a whole. We receive love in proportion to the way we give love. Harmony is the nature of love, a necessary adjunct to construction.

18. We have the equipment necessary to cope with an incarnation.

19. The circumstances of our lives are our elements of development.

20. Our daily lives must be spent acting out our beliefs if they are to benefit us.

21. Time must be spent every day in devotion, involving prayer, self-examination, thanksgiving, recollection, communication, receptivity, and awareness.

22. Daily tasks should be done in love and fully in the moment with no concern for tomorrow. If we live like this, we are putting the essential beliefs in love, faith, hope, and the goodness of God to work, and in the process we become living examples of God's will.

23. Things are not what they seem. Clear vision is a requirement for understanding.

24. Everything that happens is for the good. The good depends upon our reaction to it. All is well and as it should be.

Richard's final statement on this subject follows.

By acting on our beliefs, we become products of our beliefs. Believe what you wish, but don't expect others to believe as you do. Everyone has a right to his or her own beliefs, because it is through our own beliefs that we will develop our own life. We are all responsible for ourselves alone, and our development is up to us.

Postscript

For almost four years the doctor kept saying I should be feeling ill, but I didn't; I should feel nausea, extreme fatigue, itching, but I didn't. The doctor said that with the condition of my blood, I should be on dialysis, but he didn't want to subject me to it because I didn't have any of the symptoms. I was sure that my efforts, with help from Richard, would keep me from having to submit to the humiliation of dialysis.

I know that there are no accidents, that all events are meaningful and things are not what they seem; but it took a series of drastic experiences to teach me this.

The circumstances of my life had always been comparatively easy. Situations seemed to fall right for me, in spite of the fact that I had developed into a manic-depressive, compulsive, addictive personality.

As I read back over early communications with Richard, I can see just how much time and effort went into trying to straighten me out. "Stop worrying; faith and trust are essential. Learn to live in the moment. You must give up alcohol. Your compulsions are standing in your way." These were just some of the constant admonitions. I could go for long periods of time in relative quiet, and then something, anything, would put me right back where I started. Oh, the guilt and remorse which always followed another explosion! But I wasn't learning from my experiences. I would always go running to Richard for help after I reverted, and for a while I felt chastened, but I never faced up to my problems.

All this time I was receiving valuable information which was both intellectually and emotionally stimulating. I kept wanting to learn more, anything to get my mind off myself! I guess I thought everything would work out for me in this situation, just as it had always done in the past. But I wasn't listening. Richard kept telling me I had to learn to live out my beliefs and become an example of what I was so willing to give lip service to. It wasn't until disaster struck that I was forced to come to grips with reality.

My wife and I had talked ourselves into believing that, since peace and quiet were essential to receiving the material from Richard, we would need a place in the country, away from the hubbub of the city. In my usual compulsive manner, I searched the newspaper for advertisements for country property in New York State. We had heard from many sources about the beauty of Schoharie County (a sign!), and we finally found a beautiful piece of property, seventy-eight acres—fields, woods, ponds, streams, hills, three-quarters of a mile of private road, and not a house in sight! Perfect! Our son-in-law was studying architecture and wanted to take a year off before graduate school to design and supervise the building of the house. Everything was falling into place. I would retire and we would move to the country to do our work.

When I discussed these plans with Richard, he said I needed to continue my voice teaching for my own integration. Well, we were so sure this plan was right. After all, didn't this work deserve the best, our total attention? I did have some qualms about how I would handle so much free time, but somehow I knew everything would work out. Indeed, it did, but not as I had imagined.

For five years we traveled back and forth, spending eight hours a week in the car. Our time on either end was spent largely on chores. In the country it was the vegetable garden, the landscaping, the house, all of the minutiae which must be crowded into half a week. In the city, it meant crowding my teaching into four days with not much time for anything else. Madeleine joked that she seemed to spend most of her time in the country getting the house in order before traveling back to the city, and most of her time in the city getting the house in order before traveling back to the country. We kept thinking we would have more time for our work with Richard after things settled down. All this time Richard was telling me to stop wasting time and get down to business. I thought, "Yes, yes, of course, tomorrow." After all, weren't we doing all of this for that sole purpose? Even though we had gotten ourselves into a momentary bind, everything would be all right when I reached sixty-five and retired.

We didn't have to wait that long. One June morning in 1977, we arrived at the farmhouse to discover everything in chaos. The house had been ransacked and our new two-oven electric stove was missing along with antiques, Oriental rugs, and family heirlooms. There were enough things left, however, so that we knew we would be robbed again, and all would be lost if we didn't act immediately. We managed to get the local movers to move us on Monday morning, and we had the rest of our valuables stored, leaving just the barest minimum of furniture. We would be camping out for the rest of the summer. By the time we were able to get someone to occupy the house for us so that it wouldn't be left vacant, we had been robbed twice more, losing such things as sheets, blankets, pillows, window blinds, kitchen equipment, and cookware.

By this time our feelings of horror and chagrin and outrage at the rape of our privacy gave way to a kind of numb acceptance. We started to consider plans to have someone else live there with us indefinitely. This back-and-forth business could not continue unless we had someone else in the house. Madeleine and I valued our privacy, and the thought of sharing the space was not appealing. Maybe we'd redo the double garage into an apartment. In any case we had a tenant in the house for the winter (she had had to bring her own furniture), and we could decide what to do the following spring. We felt the success of our work depended upon this special place, and we were determined to make it work somehow.

All that year I hadn't been feeling well. I had repeated bouts with a virus, so I thought, and when I asked Richard about it, he told me not to worry, everything would be all right. The following winter found me weak but determined. Everything depended on my willingness to do the right thing. Mind over matter! Everything was really all right!

On February 1, 1978, I was rushed to the emergency room of a hospital in New York City in a state of near collapse. I had two percent kidney function with complications, pneumonia, and a pain in my chest. My life was tumbling down around me! First the sanctity of my home had been violated, and now the sanctity of my physical person was being violated. My faith in God's goodness was weakening. Was all of our effort for naught after all? Was this some kind of satanic joke?

As I lay in bed my first night in the hospital, I saw my life before me and felt God's wrath upon me. Trying to sort things out, I pleaded with Richard for help and asked, "Why did this happen to me? What can it possibly mean? Am I being punished?" Richard's answer came quickly: "It is an act of love." With this statement my eyes were drawn to the bedside lamp, and there, in the midst of this dazzling light, I saw someone looking at me. I saw just the head of a most beautiful being, with golden hair parted in the middle and large, dark eyes with the most beneficent expression I had ever seen. We held eye contact for what seemed like a long time before the vision vanished. That night as I fell asleep, I knew I was really all right in spite of appearances.

From that moment on, my fear and worry, which came from the basic insecurity which had brought on my manic-depressive moods, left me, never to return. When I left the hospital a month later, the doctor prepared me for dialysis and said it was a matter of a short time before I would require it. My kidneys had returned to fifteen percent function by then, but of course that wouldn't last long. I was sure the doctor was wrong. In the meantime, I had a tube in my bladder and would wear a leg bag until my forthcoming prostatectomy the following year. By December of 1979, I had had the operation plus a follow-up to remove blockage, was teaching a full schedule, and also had received all of the information I have recorded for this book.

I reasoned that, with my insecurity gone, I could now handle alcohol. Richard warned me about excesses, but I felt now that this was no longer a problem. I had forgotten the adage "Once an addictive nature, always an addictive nature," and without realizing the consequences, I was reverting, no matter how I justified it to myself.

Suddenly, in May 1980, the doctor reported a deterioration of my blood, which indicated that my kidneys were not holding up, and told me to prepare for the consequences. Even though he thought my kidneys were close to failing, he still needed to eliminate the infection. Since I am allergic to sulfa drugs and penicillin, he decided upon gentamicin, which I was given by injection three times a week for three weeks. By the end of the three weeks, the infection was cleared up, but the doctor thought a couple of more shots would be a good idea. The night of the last shot I developed a splitting headache, and by the next day I had vertigo—nausea, headache, and dizziness—the worst combination of sensations imaginable. When the doctor heard of my nausea (a symptom of kidney failure), he said, "That's it," and ordered me to the hospital in preparation for dialysis. However, the kidneys showed no further deterioration, and the condition was diagnosed as neurological. I had suffered nerve damage from the drug. Needless to say, I was given a barrage of tests to prove the point.

By now I began to wonder why this episode was necessary. Hadn't I learned from my previous experience? But surely I had. We had sold the farm, realizing that it represented far too much busyness. I had also realized I could never give up my teaching. By staying in the city and not wasting all that time in traveling and the minutiae of mundane matters, I found I had time for both the work and my teaching, and, in fact, the information I had received from Richard was clearer and much more succinct than any I had gotten prior to all my troubles. However, there was much more to do before the work would be completed, and I didn't feel capable of doing it. The nerve damage seemed to preclude my ever being able to finish the work that had meant so much to me.

I was devastated. If nothing is accidental, why this now? Richard reminded me I had unfinished business to clear up. When I asked for an explanation, he said, "You promised to give up alcohol and you haven't."

"But I don't need to worry about that anymore," I said. "I've overcome my insecurities."

"You went back on your word," was his answer. "You must recognize by now just how fragile your health is. It is only by the grace of God that you are not a total invalid. But since your intention has been honorable, however misguided, I will make a bargain with you. Refrain from alcohol; never touch a drop in your life again, and you will be allowed to complete this work and live in relatively good health, in spite of the way matters develop."

To the present I have been obedient to Richard's command, and through God's grace I have been able to complete this job to the best of my ability.

I am now on dialysis after all. I thought I would be able to avoid it, but not so. I can see now that the time was given me to allow me to adjust to the idea of becoming dependent upon a machine for my life.

Even with all I had learned, clarity of vision eluded me until after the fact. Richard has always told me that I need, above all else, to learn humility. For the first time in my life I am faced with a situation that I know cannot be overcome through my own efforts or anyone else's, for that matter. Because God wills it, I am dependent upon my wife and a machine for my life. I am learning the freedom of obedience, and I am thankful to God, Who has made this realization possible. Adjusting to my present situation hasn't proved to be as difficult as I had imagined it might be. I know that what I have is what I need, and but for the grace of God I would have been unable to complete this work. I have rejected the idea of a transplant because of the problems that would inevitably result from my allergies. And I know that with Richard's help I will find satisfaction in the accomplishment of things as they are. I continue to teach a full schedule and live a full life. The vertigo has virtually disappeared, and I accept my new mechanical "kidney" with gratitude and humility. I regard the machine as my best friend.

I close with a quote from Richard:

To be able to see things as they really are is essential to understanding life. Clarity of vision is often mis-understood, because things are not what they seem, and those who are content to judge events by appearances are unable to see with clarity. What they do see is hazy and therefore subject to many interpretations. In order to see clearly, we must look into the situation and find the con-struction which lies hidden. God's will is construction, and since God's will takes precedence over all else, every event, no matter how generated, no matter who the catalyst, no matter what the outcome, has within it a constructive core from which we can always learn and grow. The lessons are being taught at every turn, but if we are blind to them and don't learn from them, they will keep coming. Clarity of vision, then, is a development, and those who possess it are developed souls. The beginning of understanding is the acceptance of things as they are.